Chamomile
Field thyme
Rosehip
Big plantain
Chamomile
Field thyme

The Witch's Workshop

MELISSA JAYNE MADARA

The Witch's Workshop

A Guide to Crafting Your Own Magical Tools

WATKINS
Sharing Wisdom
Since 1893

The Witch's Workshop

Melissa Jayne Madara

First published in the UK and USA in 2024 by
Watkins, an imprint of Watkins Media Limited
Unit 11, Shepperton House, 83–93 Shepperton Road
London N1 3DF

enquiries@watkinspublishing.com

Commissioning Editor: Ella Chappell
Project Editor: Brittany Willis
Copyeditor: Sophie Elleston
Head of Design: Karen Smith
Designer: Sarah O'Flaherty
Production: Uzma Taj
Photography: Melissa Jayne Madara,
Emily Bonilla, and Dani Ellwell
Photo editing: Emily Bonilla and Dani Ellwell

Images on page 10 and 60 can be found at
WikiCommons

A CIP record for this book is available from
the British Library

ISBN: 978-1-78678-809-2 (Hardback)
ISBN: 978-1-78678-810-8 (eBook)

10 9 8 7 6 5 4 3 2 1

Typeset in Amador, Aleo and Gotham
Printed in China

Publisher's note

While every care has been taken in compiling the recipes
for this book, Watkins Media Limited, or any other persons
who have been involved in working on this publication,
cannot accept responsibility for any errors or omissions,
inadvertent or not, that may be found in the recipes or text,
nor for any problems that may arise as a result of preparing
one of these recipes. If you are pregnant or breastfeeding
or have any special dietary requirements or medical
conditions, it is advisable to consult a medical professional
before following any of the recipes contained in this book.
Some activities in this book, for example those involving
burning incense or cutting tools, may be dangerous if
instructions are not followed precisely. Always follow
manufacturers' instructions when using tools. Wild foods
such as berries can be poisonous, so eat only what you can
identify as safe. When foraging, it is likely that you will be
trying food that you have never eaten before. Therefore,
and especially if you are prone to allergies, try just a little
first, as you would with any food. The material contained
in this book is set out in good faith for general guidance and
no liability can be accepted for loss or expense incurred in
relying on the information given. In particular this book
is not intended to replace expert medical advice. This book
is for informational purposes only and is for your own
personal use and guidance. It is not intended to diagnose,
treat, or act as a substitute for professional medical advice.
Watkins Media Limited, or any other persons involved in
working on this publication, cannot accept responsibility for
any injury, illness or damages that result from participating
in the activities in this book.

watkinspublishing.com

Contents

Introduction

The Art of Green Magic

"What is a witch?" The answer to this question shapeshifts. Throughout history, we have been presented with countless images of the iconic figure of the witch, both benevolent and malevolent, springing up in all cultures which hold belief in the power of magic. We see the witch as the mossy-mouthed transgressor terrorizing the innocent, the wide-eyed sorcerer prophesying the future, and the beautiful seductress bewitching baneful elixirs, all rolled into one. Are they all-powerful Hollywood superheroes? Satanic avatars of evil on earth? Healers or poisoners? Real or imaginary? Helpful or harmful? Friend or foe? While the witch captivates our imaginations and embodies our deepest fears, they continue to elude definition, no matter how fervently we search for it.

When we turn to history for answers, surprisingly we often find the witch themselves is absent. Ideas of who and what witches have been throughout history are often given to us in secondhand sources, like witch-hunting documents, church texts on heresy, misinterpretations of natural phenomena, and descriptions of folkloric and mythological magicians. These witch-images are shared through the eyes of laypeople and non-practitioners, and historically, it's rare that we ever get to hear from witches themselves. This problem is compounded by the fact that definitions of magic shift culturally and throughout time, such that practices seen as benevolent folk charms in one century might have received a lethal sentence of heresy just a few centuries later. In these societies, magic has needed to go underground, take on new names, and survive in shadows, further obscuring the details of actual practice and discouraging practitioners from recording their work. We see echoes of this in countless traditions that use Catholic icons, like saints and angels, to safely mask devotion to illicit spirits, allowing witches to hide in plain sight. Even in cultures where magic is openly celebrated, we often inherit a hegemonic view of these religions, with the nuances of local cults and personal practice being obscured by dominant theologies. In each of these cases, history proves to be an unreliable narrator in seeking true images of magic and witchcraft.

It's important to remember that witchcraft, even as a practice that resists definition, is still distinct from other forms of magic. As a figure concerned with exploring liminality, the witch disrupts our idea of binaries, eliminating the boundaries between life and death, true and untrue, material and spiritual, in a way that is inherently transgressive. This is very different from the divine, high-magic aims of the ceremonial magicians, the chemical flash of the alchemists, or the detailed cosmological mapping of the grimoire authors. Even when it aspires to spiritual goals, witchcraft differs from all these other occult practices in that it is primarily a chthonic practice, rooted in the terrestrial, in the blood and bones and breath, and in companionship with the spirits of the land. In fact, although the witch archetype resists definition by its very nature, this interrelationship between the witch and non-human aspects of the natural world has incredibly deep roots, and is something that is not emphasized in other magical practices. This feral heart of the witch betrays a mutability between the humanness of the witch and their allyship with the wild world, conjuring images of skin turning and shapeshifting, ideas of animal familiars, and ideas of the witch as an antisocial outsider. Witches through this lens are not true members of human society, but exist on the liminal ground betwixt the material and the spiritual worlds, so closely allied with the natural world that they begin to resemble it themselves.

Of all the spirit pacts and allyships central to the witch archetype, history shows us an especially deep link between the witch and their work with plants. This is the thread that connects all images of the witch, and is emphasized again and again in defining the work of witchcraft within the Western occult. We find textual references to this connection even in the ancient world, and the emphasis on magic originating from herbs seems to be a unique feature of witchcraft in particular. Even ancient divinities who ruled the powers of witchcraft and magic, like the Greek Hekate or the Egyptian Heka, had deep associations with charms worked by herbs and plants. In particular, Hekate was regarded as the mother of prominent witches Medea and Circe, whom she was said to have tutored in magic through sharing her knowledge of herbal charms. Historically, this connection has led to much overlap between terms used to describe witches and herbalists. The Ancient Greek word for herb, *pharmakon*, can be variously translated to refer to medicinal preparations, magical concoctions, and criminals' herbal poisons. Even the word for "witch" in Latin translations of the biblical decree "suffer not a witch to live" more closely refers to a poisoner or malicious herbalist than a magical practitioner. This ambiguity creates much historical confusion over the distinction between witches and medicinal herbalists, and underscores the deep connection between witch-magic and working with plants.

Within this baseline definition of witchcraft, firmly planted within the natural world, the work of the witch occurs by and of the land they live on. This framework creates overlap between actual practitioners of magic and those who, throughout history, have possessed such a deeply intimate relationship with nature that their knowledge of its motions appears divine. In Ancient Greece, one of the most famous enchantments of all time was performed by the mythically powerful Thessalian witches, who were said to control the moon such that it could be torn from the sky, leaving a blood-red stain. This is commonly acknowledged in the modern world to have likely been the result of eclipse prediction, where Thessalian sorceresses were able to map a lunar cycle in such detail that they could make it appear as though they controlled the movements of the heavens. Many other famous charms like this illustrate the mundane origins of magical practices, always arising from intimate knowledge of nature, born of deep study and close relationship. For example, many herbs we know as cleansing and purification plants derive these associations from their antibiotic and antimicrobial properties, performing a literal cleansing of bacteria from the air when burned or steamed. Many techniques used in trance and breathwork are holy because of the physiological effects they impart upon the practitioner, which create an altered state of consciousness by lowing the heart rate and flooding the blood with oxygen. Even the rhizotomoi of Ancient Greece, the root-cutters who harvested magical and medicinal plants, observed superstitious rites and rituals that had the dual effect of appeasing plant spirits and protecting the practitioner, such as anointing the body with holy olive oil before foraging, which serves as a natural sunblock.

This deep and necessary relationship between practitioners of magic and the land they lived on was well understood throughout history, even by opponents of magic. In biblical lore, wild spaces are analogized to the uncontrollable evil of the Devil, and God is said to have given Christians divine right to subdue wild nature as an aspect of the battle for universal good. As allies of wild places and devotees of nature spirits, magical practitioners became associated with this wild evilness. When Christians of the Middle Ages sought to convert pagans, they would chop down their sacred trees and groves, destroying their connection to the land spirits in an effort toward destroying their belief.

Emil Doepler, "Bonifacius" (1905)

This anti-wild rhetoric, coupled with a historical ambiguity between witches and herbalists, likely contributed to naturopaths, midwives, and herbal doctors being accused of witchcraft in the years leading up to and during the European witch trials. These practitioners possessed a deep knowledge of natural rhythms that was dangerously challenging to the Church, and represented a firm grip of natural science, like effective weather prediction, an understanding of chemistry, medicine, and biology, and an intimate relationship with the landscape of their region. To the untrained eye, these skills appear just as bewildering and magical as the ability to cast spells. It's highly likely that many of these healers were also versed in common folk charms and forms of protection magic. This is not surprising, given that benign charms against witchcraft and misfortune were popular enough to feature in Shakespeare's plays, anticipating an audience that would have been very familiar with their use. These real-life practitioners, more likely to be called cunning persons or wise people than witches, bear little resemblance to otherworldly folkloric images of the witch. Far from being supernatural, these people were revered because they had mastered the natural secrets of the world – how to make do, and even provide wondrous results, using only the tools they had at their disposal. This multi-faceted mastery over the natural world, both mundane and metaphysical, is rarely emphasized within the mythological witch archetype, but from what history can tell us, appears to be a significant part of the lived realities of the wise and cunning people we might call witches today.

Of the land, by the land

The work of green magic within this perspective requires us to relate to nature very differently than we may be used to in the modern world. Because our current reality is so heavily influenced by the Western perspective, shaped by Christian frameworks which demonize the wild, we're not well equipped to relate to nature on a metamaterial basis. The defining paradigm of the Anthropocene takes an objectifying view of nature, as a collection of resources to be exploited for human gain in the pursuit of human desires. This perspective centers the human as the pinnacle of evolutionary progress; the only species whose needs matter,

whose voice deserves to be heard. As magical practitioners, how can we hope to forge authentic, allied relationships with nature, a requirement for the work of witchcraft, if we cannot relate to the natural world without this presumed hierarchy?

Fortunately, mystics and magical practitioners of the past can show us the way. While our current human-centric worldview can feel oppressive to those who long for deeper relationships with nature, it's important to remember that this has not always been the dominant philosophy, even in the West. In the 3rd century BCE, the Greek botanist and philosopher Theophrastus had much to say about the relationship between humans and nature. As a student of Aristotle, Theophrastus meditated on the concept of *telos*, or the idea that there is a purpose for everything that exists, and an ultimate form of existence. In plants, Theophrastus takes this to refer to the "tendency of a plant's

nature", or proper conditions of habitat, circumstance, and fate that allow a plant to reach its fullest reproductive potential. He noted that a plant's telos may be out of alignment with the telos of the greater environment, such as in the case of a plant-killing frost, a drought, or a wildfire. He further outlined how the telos of plants is frequently at odds with the human telos, citing ancient examples of deforestation and manmade erosion to illustrate his point. While this should show that the human objectification of nature is nothing new, Theophrastus also wrote extensively about plant-harvesting charms and rituals observed by the Ancient Rhizotomoi, who took great care to harvest plants such that their spirits were not offended. This arises from the belief that plants have not only intelligence and memory, but also a spiritual capacity, such that they could grant or withhold consent for being used in magical preparations. This worldview is preserved in many plant-harvesting charms of this era, which speak about plants worshipping the gods, praying, and existing as material beings with spiritual capacities, much like their human harvesters.

In the Middle Ages, St Hildegard Von Bingen, a German abbess who lived during the 11th century, introduced other novel concepts of spiritual relation to the land. While St Hildegard was certainly of a Christian perspective, her beliefs were unconventional, and arose from her frequent visions of God and His angels, which many historians attribute to her bouts of epilepsy. Among her many writings, St Hildegard uses the term viriditas, literally meaning "greenness" or "greening power", which has interesting implications for witches and animists. She takes this to refer to the power that plants have to transform the light of the sun into food and medicine, and to exist as part of the self-regulating mechanism of nature, which she saw as a "perfect" and "balanced" state of health. What's interesting about this belief is that, as a Christian, St Hildegard saw these unique properties of plants as a form of divine communication from God, with the plant kingdom being the menstruum through which He shares His love with the world by offering up nourishment and the means to heal ourselves. In this cosmology, plants are the mediators of God, divinely selected to share His blessings with the world. St Hildegard's viriditas is one of the only places in Christian theology to find plants privileged as sacred, especially existing as they are in earthbound nature, rather than in the perfected and heavenly garden portrayed in Christian theology.

Lastly, readers who study astrology may be familiar with Nicholas Culpeper, an English herbalist from the 17th century. Culpeper is most known for his democratizing of herbalism, printing affordable zines of herbal cures. These pamphlets were written in the English language, rather than the Latin used by academics, so that common people could, for

the first time, learn to cure themselves. He performed medical care for free to the lower classes, and harshly scolded his contemporaries for grifting quack cures to the poor and overcharging for their services. His outspokenness about ethical medicine in an era of great corruption led to the London Society of Apothecaries accusing Culpeper of witchcraft, in a desperate attempt to silence his voice. In addition to his activism and radical philosophy, Culpeper also practised iatromathematics, or medical astrology, using the movements of the planets and the stars to inform his diagnoses. He likened the practice of medicine without astrology to a lamp without oil, and partnered with other astrologers like William Lily to codify astrological correspondences and rulerships in planetary herbalism that are still in use by occultists today. While Culpeper is not a witch or a practitioner of magic, his perspective that herbal mastery is a human right, and that this work ought to be grounded in movements of an intelligent, heavenly macrocosm, aligns his beliefs with the core philosophies of green magic.

These three perspectives on the human/nature relationship underscore the import, both spiritual and mundane, of forming meaningful allyships with nature. In the modern world, these ideas are rare, and there are necessary consequences to those beliefs. The extractive and objectifying view of nature in the West has permitted large-scale ecological destruction, leading to our current epoch of ecological collapse. In contrast, societies built on mutually dependent views of the human–nature relationship, which anthropologist Enrique Salmon terms "kin-centric ecologies", are generally geared toward sustainability, and preserving the integrity of the entire natural system. These perspectives are usually found in indigenous cultures, which view themselves as arising from the land directly, with plants, animals, and wider ecosystems representing systems of kin, an inherited relationality with nature at large.

If we as witches want to take up the work of green magic for ourselves, stepping into these ideologies that reframe our relationship to nature will be an essential first step. This work doesn't just ground our practice in an authentically animist philosophy, but it actively works to undercut the destructive Western paradigm at the root of all environmental destruction. When we pick up this inheritance of magical wisdom, we carry forth a generative seed of possibility, demonstrating for all around that other ways of relating to the land are possible. Furthermore, with modern occultism stepping into prominence in popular culture, perspectives like these are an apotropaic charm against capitalism and the commodification of magic. As more and more witches exit the broom closet in our modern occult renaissance, more and more companies and corporations seek to profit off what they see as a trendy, viral fad, to be consumed for cheap and then discarded. In a global culture obsessed with productivity and the bottom line, an approach of slow living, hand crafting, and grounding our practice in the genius of the land is a small but important revolution. When we learn to make and craft what we need, to forge our own allyships with the land that sustains us, we show corporations that our magic is not a trend and is not for sale. It comes from a deep interconnectivity between practitioners and the spirits of the earth, which is older than capitalism, or money itself.

As a final point, this work of crafting from an animist perspective has practical benefits as well. By learning these natural arts and skills, we can achieve high degrees of transparency and specialization in crafting our magical tools and charms. For budding magical students, there can often be an impulse to look to other practitioners who we view as leaders to provide the tools and materia of our craft. We may see incredibly creative oils, incenses, and products for sale that represent a wealth of knowledge and experience that we hope to attain. However, while famous shops, influencer personalities, and high-profile community icons can of course be valuable resources for information, these figures can also use their perceived legitimacy to sell products and services with little to no transparency in their process or ingredients. This disempowers us as practitioners ourselves; we are then cut off from contact with the plant allies and spirit intelligences that make these products work. If we are to believe that our deliberateness and intentionality are driving forces for our magical practice, how can we use mass-produced ingredients or preparations in our practice when we don't know how and with what substances they are made? Not only does crafting our own tools bring this level of detail and oversight back to our work, but it allows us to create tools that are highly customized to the work at hand, instead of products for general concerns, crafted in bulk for large audiences.

How to use this book

In this book, you will explore several botanical crafts and procedures as an effort toward forging these direct, allied relationships with plants and your local environment. Through experimenting with making incense, natural dyes, inks, papers, candles, oils and powders, you will master the skills to craft your own magical tools. Try your hand at a selection of my own recipes to get you started. Many other recipes will be pulled from historical

sources, putting us in touch with the magical perspectives of witches past and investigating novel approaches to both crafting and magic. These recipes come from my personal research into European occult history, which focuses on plant folklore and the magical traditions of the Mediterranean coast, my ancestral homeland. While the scope of this research and the examples we explore is necessarily narrow, examples of these kinds of charms and botanical crafts can be found in every magical culture on earth, well beyond the limits of European history alone.

Through the recipes and spells in this book, it is my hope to put readers in touch with an ancestral language – a silent tongue of pigment, perfume, and chemical flux – in an effort toward healing our severed relationship with the spirits of the natural world. These formulas will encourage you to explore your environment high and low, seeking out the magical herbs and unmet allies that undoubtedly wait just beyond your front door. For witches and practitioners with a grounding in magic, this book will demonstrate new techniques in a way that can be tailored to suit the beliefs, strengths, and skills of your current practice. For those approaching witchcraft for the first time through this book, I encourage you to dive into these pages with a radical sense of play, keeping an open mind as you begin to develop your own ideas of what practising magic means. In either case, this book is a spell, a portal, and an initiation into the world of green magic, and I hope that you follow this crooked path as far as it can take you.

Preparing the verdant altar

In taking up this work for ourselves, we leave the safe nucleus of theory and enter the fraught, vulnerable realm of practice. If you're new to magic or are just exploring

these tools for the first time, it's normal to feel unsteady in your footing. Remaining as "armchair witches" preserves us against disappointment and self-doubt, but it's important to ground our beliefs in actionable praxis, to sometimes "get our fingers burned", as occultist Jake Stratton-Kent often said. Other authors like chaos magician Phil Hine emphasize direct practice as the route to comprehending magic on a visceral level, analogizing witchcraft to sex, in that both practices need to be physically experienced in order to be fully understood. The costs of leaving the idealized, intellectual realm of study are high, and leaving the comfort zone makes our fumbles, foibles, and missteps uncomfortably visible to the outside world. However, since magic is conditional and subjective, not existing in perfect objectivity outside ourselves, forging our own magical relationships and crafting our own tools puts us in touch with the only expert we will ever need, the self, and the highly specialized tools of our minds, bodies, and spirits.

However, there are a few helpful tools and tips that can give us more grounding in navigating new magical technologies. Whether you're new to magic and apothecary sciences, or seeking to develop an existing practice, there are a few subjects which could use some explanation to help readers make the most of their time, resources, and crafting experiences.

Sourcing botanicals

In the recipes ahead, you will be called to work with plants in a variety of methods, using dried, fresh, powdered, and extracted herbs to create an array of specialized magical tools. As the plants themselves will be the primary media for this creative work, it's important to source high-quality botanicals from trusted retailers or from our environment in order to achieve the best results. While growing our own herbs and flowers offers the highest degree of quality and oversight, many readers may find themselves without gardening space, or unable to grow specific exotic plants called for in these charms, like cardamom, lemongrass, frankincense, or clove. In these cases, sourcing our plants from trusted herb shops and online retailers is our best option, though it is also the most expensive choice, with the largest negative environmental impact. Whether you live in the city or the country, you may also be surprised to find a large number of these plants growing in your own backyard. In these cases, foraging your own botanicals may be the best opportunity to source fresh, healthy plants while minimizing your costs and carbon footprint. This work puts us directly in touch with the land we live on, and will be worth exploring for those who seek congress with their local genii loci, or spirits of place. However, there are three important guidelines to keep in mind while foraging for wild plants:

* **POINTS OF ID** – When foraging for plants in the wild, it's important to be able to identify plant allies by multiple features, so we can be sure we've found exactly what we're looking for. As a general rule, you should notice at least three points of identification (leaf shape, fragrance, flower colour, bioregion, etc.) on a plant in order to make a positive ID in the field. For example, many readers can likely find the tenaciously weedy mugwort plant growing nearby, which can be identified by its deeply "toothed" and jagged leaves with silver undersides, its small buds of aromatic flowers, purple late-season stems, and its presence along roadways, park edges, and other wayside areas.

* **SAFE GATHERING ZONES** – While we may often spot beautiful flowers and wild herbs springing up throughout our neighborhoods, there is good reason to be cautious about where we choose to forage. Unfortunately, environmental toxins are a serious concern for wild plants, and many of these botanicals absorb dangerous pollutants and heavy metals like lead, cadmium, and arsenic into their bodies from contaminated soil. The best way to ensure that our soils are free from damaging toxins is to have them tested by a lab, a service offered through many universities and soil-testing programmes. Otherwise, foragers in these spaces can keep themselves safer by only picking plants which grow a minimum of 20 yards (about 18m) from man-made structures, such as roads, sidewalks, lamp posts, buildings, railings, and fences.

* **HONOURABLE HARVEST** – As witches working with plants from an allied, animistic perspective, it's important to be good guests when we find ourselves in wild places. Understanding that we are gathering from living, autonomous spirits puts greater pressure on the need for ethical and honourable harvesting practices, which are grounded in energetic exchange. This often takes the form of making and leaving generous offerings to plant spirits and spirits of the land, such as food, wine, fertilizer, song, prayer, or even just the tending of a devoted relationship. More practically, this means we are conservative in how much we choose to harvest from a particular patch of plants, making sure we only take what we are certain that we will use. As a general rule, consider harvesting no more than a third

of the plants you see in a given area at any time. Should you return to the same patch twice, harvest a maximum one third of the remaining bounty, so that the other spirits of these wild places, particularly birds, animals, and insects who rely on these plants, can have their due share as well.

Tools of the arte

One of the most beautiful things about the apothecary sciences is how accessible they are to practise, requiring very little investment in equipment. As green magic is a decidedly domestic art, it's likely you already have many helpful tools at home. When building your own home apothecary, there are a few key tools you will want to make sure you have on hand, as well as some guidelines for their use:

* **GRINDING, CHOPPING & CUTTING TOOLS** – These tools will be important for harvesting and processing your plants to make them usable in craft work. When harvesting, sharp blades and clean cuts will cause the least distress to plants, and allow them to heal and regrow, enabling successive harvests. In processing plants, scissors or herb choppers are a helpful tool for roughly processing fresh plants, while mortar and pestles may be more suited to breaking down dry botanicals. As modern practitioners, using electric chopping tools like blenders, food processors and spice grinders goes a long way, but we want to be sure we're using these tools only for edible plants if we plan to repurpose them in our cooking as well.

* **MIXING BOWLS & STORAGE VESSELS** – Proper storage of plants and preparations will extend their shelf life and allow us to reap greater benefits from our work.

Mixing bowls and storage jars should always be made of non-reactive materials, like glass, Pyrex, or ceramic, with plastic and wood being the two least favourable materials. In addition, airtight storage vessels will work wonders against humidity, pests, and temperature changes, which can significantly degrade the quality of our herbs and mixtures.

* **STRAINERS, FILTERS & SIEVES** – Many of the recipes ahead will require us to make infusions and fine plant powders, which use filters and sieves. These tools allow us to clarify and strain liquid preparations, while preventing lumps and caking in powders and dry blends. Your home apothecary should have a mix of these tools, ranging from wide-holed colanders and tamises to sieves/fine-mesh strainers, cheesecloths and coffee filters.

* **GLOVES & PERSONAL PROTECTION EQUIPMENT** – While all the crafts ahead are safe to complete at home, certain preparations require us to take precautions. Take care to read the steps and notes for all recipes, as some may recommend using gloves and face masks, or working within ventilated areas, to protect you from irritants, stains, fumes, and burns.

* **SEPARATE TOOLS FOR APOTHECARY WORK** – Because many of the recipes ahead call for inedible ingredients, such as essential oils, plasters, metallic salts, and wood powders, it's important that all apothecary tools remain separate from our kitchen equipment, and not be used to prepare food. This goes for all equipment, from small mixing spoons to large storage jars and vessels. Thankfully, most of these tools are easy to find and quite affordable, requiring only a small investment in core equipment in order to get started.

In addition to the tools mentioned here, some recipes and crafts may require specialized equipment, like a mould and deckle for shaping paper, or a mallet for making ecoprints. Many of these can be found around the home, such as saucepans and twine, but take care to read all the steps for each recipe before beginning to ensure that you have all the required tools and ingredients on hand.

Using your resources

While this book spends lots of time exploring the magic of historical spells, living in the modern world is a beautiful thing. At this point in history, we are afforded the great wonders of the internet and digitized libraries, putting us in touch with millennia of knowledge and research on witchcraft and plants. For all that we can learn from direct experience with nature, there's an additional wealth of knowledge to be found in learning from practitioners of the past, whose unique challenges and perspectives may offer ideas we otherwise would never encounter. This is especially true in connecting with animist herbalists of the past, particularly Black and Indigenous practitioners whose work arises from intimate relationships with the plants and the land. These voices and ways of interacting with nature are largely obscured from modern herbalist discourse, robbing us as practitioners of so much helpful research and scholarship. I highly encourage readers to seek out writing and resources from these perspectives, especially those which are tied to the land you live and work upon, as an important measure in developing your personal craft.

Incense

Incense

Whether by rosemary, myrrh, crushed berries, or fresh blood, the world of the witch is a fragrant one. Magic is both guided by and rooted in the sensory and somatic, so the witch-world is naturally one that excites the senses toward their limits. But among the senses of the body, it is the sense of smell which has the deepest and closest relationship to magic. This command of fragrance as a ritual tool has been a cornerstone of magico-religious practice since the ancient world, and is exemplified nowhere more beautifully than in the production of handmade incense.

Since the earliest sorcerers in the most ancient civilizations, fragrance has played a key role in the spiritual and magical practices of witches. In Ancient Mesopotamia, a woman now known only as Tapputi served as the world's first recorded chemist and perfumer, and was given high royal status for her skills. Tapputi's special command of fragrances infused from tree resins, flowers, and roots granted her religious authority as well as her blends (such as Tapputi's Royal Salve from page 190) were consecrated under the full moon and crafted through communion with the stars. Both of the earth and of the heavens, these blends, and the honours Tapputi received for creating them, emphasize how precious fragrance was as a religious technology in Mesopotamian magic. We see similar trends in other ancient civilizations as well, such as in Egypt and Greece, where scent and fragrance were key components of both devotional worship and practical magic.

But advanced distillations and extractions like Tapputi's would not be widely available for some thousands of years, and in these furthest reaches of history, specialized ritual fragrance almost always referred to incense or burned plants. Even the origins of the word perfume – per (from) and fume (smoke) – hint at these origins. Incense altars had central positions within the temples of Ancient Greek and Jewish religion, upon which fragrant offerings could be burned. In Ancient Egypt, the iconic fragrance of kyphi incense (see page 50), made from spicy herbs and dried honey, billowed from temples at dusk. In one of the most famous examples of magical smoke, Apollo's oracle at Delphi in Ancient Greece reportedly made her prophecies from atop a golden tripod seat, surrounded by the incense of burning bay leaves, Apollo's most sacred plant, and astride a chasm which billowed psychotropic volcanic gasses. Her powerful visions were attributed to the mingling of these sacred, aromatic fumes.

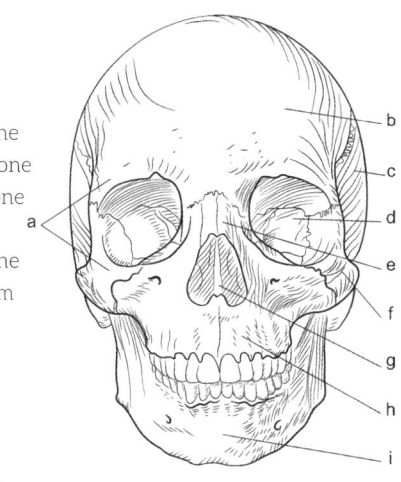

a. Orbit
b. Frontal bone
c. Temporal bone
d. Sphenoid bone
e. Nasal bone
f. Zygomatic bone
g. Nasal septum
h. Maxilla
i. Mandible

From these various examples, it's easy to see that throughout magical history incense performs a unique and essential function. As a ritual technology, incense is favoured for its ability to pierce and permeate between the physical and non-physical worlds. The fragrant smoke exists both physically and non-physically, visible and then invisible, everywhere and nowhere at once, detectable only through scent. For this reason, incense is frequently seen in rituals of communion with spirits, as the fire consumes the physical incense and lifts it heavenward, to the mysterious subtle realms of the Otherworld. In this way, incense is also a method for suffusing the powers of plants and resins into our spaces, our clothing, and our bodies, often acting as an important vehicle of consecration. Pythagoras is famously credited with introducing libanomancy to Greece, or the process of divination by scrying on incense smoke. And while many ancient cultures emphasize plant resins as the basis for incense, the burning of fragrant leaves is also common around the world, such as the Ancient Egyptian practice of burning bouquets of flowers as incense, similar to the Scottish practice of saining with burning rowan and juniper, or the white sage smudges found in many indigenous religions of North America.

However, there are also mundane, meat-and-bones explanations for why our sense of smell is particularly favoured in magic and religion. Within the structure of the human skull, our brains directly interact with the outside world in one special place – the ethmoid bone, a perforated part of the skull within our nose that allows fragrance molecules to enter the brain directly. On top of the ethmoid bone sits our olfactory bulb, at a point just between the eyes and behind the nose bridge. While our other senses – touch, sight, hearing, and taste – are routed into the brain through the thalamus, the main stimulus-processing centre of the brain, scent takes a different pathway. As scent molecules enter our brains and are processed by the olfactory bulb, they are routed through two organs before they reach the thalamus – the amygdala and the hippocampus, which regulate memories and emotional responses, and even physiological responses to emotions, such as laughing when happy or crying when sad. Because of this different processing pathway, one could say scent is "felt" before it is "thought" – in other words, we form emotional impressions about fragrance before we consciously apprehend it. This is also why scent is often the most complicated sense to describe, often relying on a synesthesia of other senses to approximate the experience, such that fragrances can be described as "sweet" without having flavour, or "heavy" without having weight.

Interestingly, without any knowledge of the brain's biochemical processing pathways, this distinction about scent was understood even in the ancient world and imbued this sense with a greater spiritual capacity than perhaps any other. In Ancient Greece, plants with more potent scents were believed to be more medicinally and magically valuable, such as the sweet fruits of the mandrake plant or aromatic tree resins like frankincense and myrrh. In Ancient Egypt, sacred aromatic oils were anointed upon statues and bodies of the dead by tracing these fragrances across the lower forehead, anointing the scent-processing part of the brain with perfumes. In addition, ancient religions frequently related scent to experiences of the divine, with different scents said to please or displease divinity, or to possess the power to unlock greater capacity for gnosis. Scent itself was often viewed as a sign of contact with the divine, with gods and goddesses believed to leave behind sweet and delicious fragrances when they appeared on earth, such as the overwhelming floral fragrance of the "miracle of the roses", which continues to accompany apparitions of the Virgin Mary in Catholic cults even today.

In this chapter, several unique historical examples of incense magic will be presented, putting us in touch with this deep lineage of witches' fragrances. We'll experience the aromas of ancient spells, and craft our own incense blends inspired by the magic of long ago. To do this, we'll need to take a deep look at four different incense-crafting techniques: the making of loose incense, as well as sticks, cones, and pearls. These methods share similar chemical characteristics but are blended in different ratios to create incenses which function according to the needs of the magician.

Among the four incense-crafting methods we will look at in this chapter, there are two main categories – direct-burning (combustible) incense, and indirect-burning (non-combustible) incense. Direct-burning blends, like incense sticks and cones, are ones which continue to hold a flame after you light them, and burn on their own to completion. This is due to the presence of two specialized ingredients – a binder and a combustion agent – which help these blends burn autonomously. Indirect-burning blends, like loose incense or incense pearls, do not include combustion agents and therefore require a constant external heat source to burn, which is usually a hot charcoal. These little charcoal briquettes are like those used for hookah, also known as shisha, and can be purchased at most smoke shops, herb stores, or online. This is the way incense was burned for most of human history, and when we look at historical recipes for incense, they will almost always require indirect-burning methods.

All four of these incense types are made up of similar botanical ingredients: herbs, seeds, woods, and resins. Even the special ingredients required for direct-burning blends are all-natural and plant-based. Binders can be made of either powdered resins like acacia or xanthan gum, or sticky woods like makko, joss, and marshmallow roots. Combustion agents are typically wood powders, such as sandalwood, cedar, agarwood, or quassia, which burn hot enough to serve as the fuel for our incense. You may have expected to see fragrances or essential oils on this list of ingredients, but these will always be left out of incense recipes. The heat from burning plants will alter or destroy any fragrance extracts we add, so it's

best to save these costly ingredients for projects where they can truly shine.

Incense tools

There are certain tools you will need for crafting incense, regardless of which style you choose.

* **GRINDING & PROCESSING TOOLS** – Because all incense blends need finely chopped herbs and resins, grinding tools like a mortar and pestle, food processor, or spice grinder will be of the utmost importance. For processing dense woods like palo santo, tools like wood files, woodworking graters, or rasps will also be handy.

* **MIXING TOOLS** – You will also need mixing bowls, gloves, and rubber spatulas for blending your incense.

* **BAKING PARCHMENT/GREASEPROOF/ WAX PAPER** – For drying cones, pearls, and sticks.

* **AIRTIGHT JARS** – For storing incense long term.

* **SCALE** – For making precise measurements of ingredients.

If you plan to make stick incense, you will also need bamboo splits, which can be ordered online from incense supply shops. Cone incense may require a cone mould for shaping, as well as a small pin for poking an air hole to help the cones burn. Some incense recipes, like the ancient kyphi incense, require a saucepan to simmer incense herbs in wine. Read each recipe carefully before beginning to ensure you have all required tools and ingredients on hand.

How to make incense

You can find detailed step-by-step instructions in the recipe pages that follow, but the basic procedure for making incense is very simple. Of the four different incense types in this chapter, loose incense will be the easiest for beginners to master. This style of incense follows a simple ingredient ratio and requires as few as two ingredients to prepare. Loose incense can also be made very quickly and is the only one of the four types in this chapter that can be crafted for immediate use. If you are new to making incense, you should consider testing new blends as loose incenses first, so that you can perfect your fragrance profile before adding other ingredients like water, binders, or combustion agents into the mix.

Direct-burning blends may sound intimidating at first, but they rely on basic chemistry that anyone can understand. For incense to produce a fragrant, perfumed smoke, it needs to smoulder rather than burn. In indirect-burning blends, resin performs this function, liquefying at the touch of heat to surround the fragrant herbs and woods, allowing them to smoulder and release their fragrance slowly. But in direct-burning blends, which are moulded and shaped, a liquid resin would cause our cones or sticks to melt before they burned, and with no external heat source, these blends would snuff themselves out quickly. For this reason, direct-burning blends require both a binder and a combustion agent, to hold our shapes together, and to act as fuel for incense sticks and cones to burn to completion.

Incense pearls, a favoured method of shaping incense from Ancient Egypt through the Middle Ages, are made almost identically to incense sticks and cones, but require no specialized ingredients. Instead, resin binders like acacia, finely powdered frankincense, or xanthan gum help the botanicals come together into a dough, which can be rolled into pearls by hand. Like loose incense, these precious pearls will need a lit charcoal in order to burn. While working with charcoal may be intimidating to some, using proper censors and tongs will make the process simple, and because indirect-burning incenses require no additional ingredients, the quality of your fragrance will speak for itself.

The incense blends that you create can be made of any herbs, woods, or resins you like, but the best results will be from plants which are very aromatic. Fragrant evergreens, perfumed flowers, and essential oil-rich seeds are strong contenders for incense blends. In the case of direct-burning blends, some ingredients will already be chosen for you out of necessity. Each binder and combustion agent will have its own subtle scent, so it will be important to choose ingredients for these blends that are harmonious with the fragrance you want to achieve. However, it is important to note a plant's fragrance will always change when burned, so experimentation with different herbs and resins will be key to refining your recipes.

Which type of blend should you choose to make? All four different styles certainly have benefits and drawbacks. Moulding cones, sticks, and pearls are time-consuming, but result in a more unified fragrance with an attractive appearance. On the other hand, loose incense blends allow for a high degree of customizability. Indirect-burning blends have a longer historical tradition of use and can be made rather quickly, while direct-burning blends are more convenient to use and require no censors or charcoal to burn. These considerations will determine what style of incense you choose to make, but a mastery of each of these methods will grant the witch true mastery of the art, and give them the tools to customize their magical scentcraft to perfection.

Below, you will find step-by-step instructions for crafting incense pearls, cones, sticks, and powders. Follow these steps closely to create your own custom blends, or experiment with one of the recipes given on the next few pages.

STEP 1 –
Decide on the purpose for your blend

As with any magical act, it's best to begin by narrowing our aims to a pin-focus. After all, in order to head toward our destination, we must first be clear about where we're going. Whether you're crafting incense for ritual, spellwork, celebration, or fragrance, you should spend some time in meditation on what you hope to achieve with your blend. Consider carefully your vision for the scent, intention, and composition. Should the fragrance be pronounced or subtle? Flower-forward or of the earth? What spirits or allies should be considered in your crafting? Do any ingredients need to be dried, foraged, or purchased? Do you have time to dry and cure your blend into sticks, or should it be an off-the-cuff loose incense powder? Remember that true intentionality involves following a pure creative vision, so craft yours carefully before you move forward if you want to achieve the best results.

It is also worthwhile to bring intentionality to the nature of the ingredients you use in your blend, and this may require the witch to plan their work ahead of time. As opposed to other magical preparations, it's important to note that incense is only made with dried plant materia, as wet resins or soft roots simply will not burn. If you're harvesting your own plants for incense, remember to dry them thoroughly for at least two weeks before use. If you cannot grow or harvest your own herbs, be sure to purchase from reputable dealers – especially in the case of incense resin, which can sometimes be fake or very poor quality if purchased without care. You should also take care to properly time the harvesting of plants and the crafting of your incense blend with respect for magical and astrological alignments. Historically, herbs which are picked or tools that are crafted on specific holidays, such as Hexennacht ("Witch's Night", 30 May) or Midsummer (summer solstice, 20–21 June), will hold greater capacity as magical allies, and will offer greater potential when used for our work. Be mindful of astrological transits, sabbats, and planetary-harvesting guides in picking your plants and mixing your herbs and use these currents to their greatest potential.

STEP 2 –
Select your herbs

With your heart set to the aim of your work, it's time to select your plant allies. For practical spellwork, I find that determining the ruling planet of your operation is a good first step, from which all else follows. For example, to make incense for a love spell, with "love" being under the rulership of Venus, we should select plants that are also under Venus' designation, like roses, mints, and aromatic seeds like fenugreek and cardamom. Feel free to consult the chart of planetary correspondences on pages 220–1 for a sense of what spells, themes, and concepts fall under the rulership of different planets. You can select your herbs from within these categories, focusing on plants that are fragrant and aromatic.

If your blend is being crafted for a particular ritual or sabbat, you may want to see if there are any herbs or smells which are sacred for those occasions. Particularly when using incense as an offering to spirits, you can often find lists of traditional offerings and rulerships that can give you a clue as to what plants and fragrances might be appropriate. For example, we know that myrrh is a resin used in the rituals of Hekate in Ancient Greece, so we can use myrrh in devotional incense blends for Hekate. Blackberries are traditional in celebrations of the Autumn Equinox, so we may choose to use blackberry leaf and other seasonal allies in celebration of that solar holiday. A combination of folkloric uses, planetary correspondences, traditional ingredients, and intuitive selection should determine the herbs you use, but as always, take your time to make decisions deliberately and intentionally using all the resources you have.

No matter what the purpose of your blend, you will want to make sure you have enough herbs on hand to craft your incense properly. There are two tried-and-true incense ratios in this chapter that can help guide your ingredient selection process; one for direct-burning blends and one for indirect-burning blends. These ratios are by weight, meaning each herb will need to be weighed and measured carefully to achieve a proper blend. For example, to make a 57g (2oz) batch of incense, we will need to gather the following:

DIRECT BURNING

34g/1.2oz combustion agent
17g/0.6oz fragrant botanicals
6g/0.2oz binding agent

INDIRECT BURNING

40g/1.4oz resins and gums
17g/0.6oz fragrant botanicals

STEP 3 –
Grind or process your plant material

At this point, it's time to get to work! If you buy your dried herbs from shops or online, it's likely that they have already been cut, sifted, and processed into smaller pieces to make them easier to work with. If the pieces of the herb are about as fine as grains of rice, these herbs are likely already broken down enough for most loose incense blends. However, if you're looking to make stick, pearl, or cone incense, you'll want to process your herbs down to a fine powder. I find that an herb chopper or food processor should be strong enough to break down most plants, but for denser herbs like seeds, barks, roots, or berries, a mortar and pestle or electric spice grinder may be necessary. This grinding step will be important for your resins, which need to be broken down as finely as possible in order to properly melt in our incense once lit. To ensure your blend is evenly mixed, it's important to process each of your ingredients separately before combining them together into the final incense.

For a loose incense blend, you may process your herbs as coarsely or finely as you like. A coarse grind, to rice-sized grains, will allow us to make blends which burn for longer and can be thrown together quickly. Powdered herbs will burn more quickly on the coal, but will produce a more singular, unified fragrance. Once your herbs are measured and processed, add them to a large non-porous mixing bowl (metal, glass, ceramic, or silicone preferred). Because incense resins become sticky when mixed, I find it helpful to use gloves or rubber spatulas for the following steps. Be sure to work in an area that is easy to clean, and if you struggle to tidy up dried resins after the mixing process, remember that these can be easily dissolved with high-proof alcohol: isopropyl, ethanol, vodka, or whatever you have on hand.

STEP 4 –
Mix your blend together

Next, it's time to mix our blend. Following the ratios given on page 33, blend your processed herbs in a bowl large enough to contain your final mixture. Use your hands or a spoon to mix the herbs together until evenly blended. If you are making a loose incense blend, add a few teaspoons of a neutral carrier oil, such as coconut, grapeseed, or almond oil, and mix into your blend until it achieves a wet sand consistency, or until a hand pressed into the mixture leaves an indent behind. This carrier oil will begin to interact with your resin, softening it and allowing it to infuse into the herbs of your incense. Oils with low smoke points, such as olive, sunflower, or walnut oil, should not be used as carrier oils.

If you are making stick, cone, or pearl incense, use water to activate your binder instead. Add your water slowly, only one teaspoon at a time, until your powdered

ingredients form a smooth, pliable dough. If you accidentally add too much water, allow your dough to stand uncovered for 15–20 minutes to dry out. When the dough is at a workable consistency, like tacky clay, you may begin shaping your incense.

Cones and pearls can be shaped by hand, but incense sticks will require thin bamboo skewers, or "splits", to shape them properly. To shape your sticks, roll a thin log of your incense dough to a length that is just shorter than your wooden split. Rolling back and forth with your fingers, work the dough into an even thickness, and then place your split alongside the thin strip of dough. Gently roll the two together, back and forth, until the split is fully and evenly encased. These finished incense sticks, as well as freshly moulded cones or pearls, can be set on greaseproof paper to dry for at least 1 week before using them.

INCENSE RATIOS

DIRECT-BURNING BLENDS
sticks & cones

❦

60 per cent combustion agent
30 per cent fragrant botanicals
10 per cent binding agent

INDIRECT-BURNING BLENDS
pearls & loose incense

❦

70 per cent resins and gums
30 per cent fragrant botanicals

STEP 5 –
Dry and cure

Finally, our incense needs to dry and cure. This final step is not mandatory for loose incense but will yield a product that is much richer and more cohesive than it would otherwise be. Once prepared, and in the case of stick, cone, and pearl incense fully dried, our incense blends benefit from a curing process for at least 2–4 weeks. This step allows the resins to soften and seep into the dry plants, further unifying the fragrance of the blend. If your incense ever smells too smoky, acrid, or campfire-like the first time you burn it, this curing step will remove or greatly soften this unpleasant smell, allowing more delicate notes to develop.

To cure your incense, seal it in an airtight container and store in a cool, dry place for 2 weeks to 1 month, or as long as you like. Like wine, incense blends will change and shift over time, revealing more complexity and depth with age if stored properly. However, if stored improperly, incense can lose its fragrance entirely, so it's important to always store our blends out of direct sunlight, away from sources of heat, and in sealed, airtight containers.

STEP 6 – Light

Congratulations, your first incense blend is ready to be sampled! Always make sure to burn your incense in a proper burner or heatproof dish, no matter what kind of blend you've made. If you've chosen to make incense sticks or cones, you can hold a lighter or open flame to the tip of your incense, allow a coal to form, and blow out the flame before setting the incense into a burner. Take note of how well the blend holds the flame, and if it burns all the way through or goes out on its own. Does it hold its shape? Is the fragrance how you like it? If not, make notes on your blend for the next attempt. Add more combustion agent to increase burnability, and experiment with new ratios of botanicals until you get the fragrance just so.

For loose or pearl incense, you will need to light a charcoal. To do this, follow the method opposite.

1 Using chopsticks or tongs, grasp a single charcoal brick and hold it close to a lighter or open flame until it begins to spark.

2 When the sparks begin to spread across the coal, set it into its censer or dish.

3 Once the coal is lit and no longer sparking, place your incense into the divot in the coal's centre.

4 Wait a few seconds for the resins to melt, and when the smoke begins to rise, your incense is lit!

5 You may need to refresh the incense as it burns through, but most coals have a burn time of 45 minutes to 1 hour, allowing you to produce much more smoke and fragrance with these blends than their direct-burning cousins.

As you move through the recipes ahead, you may find you have an affinity or preference for one incense style over another. If you see a recipe you like, consider adapting the blend to suit your favourite incense method. While each formula in this chapter is written for a specific incense style, I encourage you to experiment with the fragrances within these blends, swapping out aromatics and herbs to suit your preferences and make these recipes your own.

HOME BLESSING INCENSE

The homes of witches seem to possess a powerful mythical allure, and for good reason. From Baba Yaga's chicken-footed hut to the reclusive towers of fairytale witches, it's clear to see that the place where the witch lives is where the magic happens! For this reason, rituals to bless, consecrate, and purify homes are among the most ancient in the world, and many of these charms emphasize the use of smoke.

This home blessing blend is a quick-crafting loose incense which focuses on domestic peace and protection, using accessible, easy-to-find aromatics that may already be hiding in your kitchen. Herbs like rosemary and juniper are associated with domestic peace, while bay and fennel are potent herbs of protection magic and transformation. Our primary resin for this blend, frankincense, is a natural antidepressant, which purifies the new space with its rich fragrance. It is worth noting, as we craft a blend that will bless our new home and hearth, that all of these plants are edible – yes, even frankincense! If you are planning to work this recipe, please take note of your timing, as you should begin this charm on the evening of the full moon.

Makes: 35g/1.23oz loose incense
Prep time: 20 minutes, plus overnight and 1 month curing

FOR THE INCENSE
* 1 teaspoon good-quality oil
* 21g/0.74oz frankincense resin
* 3g/0.11oz juniper berry
* 3g/0.11oz dried rosemary
* 1g/0.04oz bay leaf
* 2g/0.07oz fennel seed
* Grinding and processing tools (see page 28)
* Mixing bowl
* Airtight jar

1 Leave your oil under the light of the full moon overnight.

2 The very next day, grind/process all the botanical ingredients to your desired coarseness, but no piece should be larger than a grain of rice.

3 Place these in a mixing bowl, then add the moon oil and stir to combine all ingredients evenly.

4 Transfer the incense to an airtight jar and cure for 1 month, or until the full moon rises again.

5 For the ritual, once you have fully moved into your new space, open every door and window (this includes closets, drawers, cabinets, and crawlspaces). Light a charcoal in a censor that can be carried in your hands, and once lit, place a small heap of your incense powder on top. When the smoke begins to rise, carry this censor room to room, making sure the smoke is waved into every corner, crack, and crevice. Accompany this fumigation with song, either in a long, rising intonation of notes that vibrate off the walls of the home, or with the lyrics to a loud, joyful song that you love. The purpose of this ritual action is to fill the space with a sonic blast from deep within your core, allowing your voice, along with the incense smoke, to fill your space completely. With this in mind, select a meaningful oration from your practice or list of favourite songs that represents the joyful, harmonious, and grounded energy you wish to bring into the new home. There will be no corner where shadows can hide or despair can linger, as your words and the perfumed smoke of your magic chases every shade and ghost from the space.

PURIFICATION INCENSE CONES

There is an important distinction between cleansing and purification in magic. These words often come hand in hand, but as magical operations, they are not interchangeable. While cleansing magic focuses on the removal of particular influences, purification is concerned with returning something to a "right state" of being. This emphasis is not concerned with a moral binary, or removing "negative" influences, but with removing anything that obscures a pure state of being. This definition may sound esoteric, but looking at the herbal actions of these plants may give us deeper insight into how this magic works.

It's no secret that there is great correspondence between the magical and medicinal uses of plants. Herbs that perform aphrodisiac actions are often associated with love magic and herbs that help us sleep are often associated with bringing dreams. Herbs that are used for magical purification are no different. These plants are often those with a pleasing, fresh aroma (no cloying roses or rank valerian here), whose fragrance has uplifting, soothing qualities. This is not purely subjective, and the fragrance of many of these herbs

has been substantiated as a natural antidepressant by modern science. Purifying plants are also typically those with anti-inflammatory and antimicrobial properties, which cleanse the air of sickness and disease. When we consider what kind of forces might keep us from being fully ourselves, or from being in a "right state" of being, sickness and depression are usually at the top of the list. While these are just the mundane chemical properties of these herbs, we know as witches that what occurs on earth will be mirrored in heaven, and that what we set in motion outside of ourselves will always turn the wheels of change within.

As purification magic is a foundational part of good spiritual hygiene, this recipe is useful to keep on hand, and will be an easy way to practise your skills with crafting direct-burning incense. These purification cones use accessible, inexpensive aromatics in a very small batch so that you can troubleshoot your blending skills. Remember that grinding, mixing, shaping, and drying are all critical for incense cones, and honing your technique with each of these steps will help your incense come out just so.

Makes: 10–20 incense cones
Prep time: 1 hour, plus 3 weeks drying and 1 month curing

FOR THE INCENSE

* 17g/0.6oz palo santo or cedar wood
* 2g/0.07oz bay leaf
* 4g/0.14oz angelica root
* 1 tablespoon frankincense resin
* 2g/0.07oz dried juniper berries or fronds
* 3g/0.1oz makko powder
* Grinding and processing tools (see page 28)
* Mixing bowl
* Water
* Cone mould (optional)
* Pin/thin nail

* Baking parchment/greaseproof/wax paper
* Airtight jar

1 Finely grind/process all the botanical ingredients. For the palo santo or cedar wood, small chips can be ground in a spice grinder, but larger pieces can be turned into sawdust using a wood rasp or woodworking grater.

2 Place these powders in a mixing bowl and mix to combine. Little by little, add small quantities of water and stir until a smooth dough forms. This dough should be pliable, but still able to hold its shape.

3 Using your hands or a cone mould, gently press the dough

into a cone shape about 2.5cm/1in tall, then use a pin or thin nail to poke a hole from the bottom of the cone to the tip – not far enough to poke through, but enough to create an aeration channel through the cone. This will help the incense to burn.

4 Dry these cones on baking parchment or greaseproof paper for at least 3 weeks, then cure in an airtight jar for 1 month.

5 Burn for rites of cleansing and purification, especially on the full moon, wafting the smoke through your space, across your whole body, or over any objects (such as Tarot cards) that need to be cleansed.

FULL MOON INCENSE PEARLS

The full moon is a powerfully iconic image that has been synonymous with witchcraft and magic since the very ancient world. The moon was the emblem of ancient goddesses like Hekate and Diana who were believed to instruct their devotees in magic and herbcraft, and the medieval witches were said to gather for their sabbatic rites under the full moon's shining rays. In astrology and planetary magic, the moon in her fullest state is the highest expression of lunar virtue, ruling the arts of divination, dreams, necromancy, and potent powers of magical manifestation. It is during this phase at the climax of the lunar cycle that the moon shines the brightest, pulls the strongest upon the tides, and exerts her greatest influences upon the lives of humans beneath her glow.

This blend calls upon five lunar herbs, chosen for their deep history of association with the moon and lunar magic. These are very gentle, accessible herbs which produce an aromatic incense with a light, green, and resinous fragrance. The optional ingredients in this recipe will be more difficult to source and do not greatly assist in the fragrance of this blend, but help to lend additional layers of significance to our incense. Lotus stamens, if included, will be the only aquatic plant in this blend, calling upon the moon's rulership of watery places. By rolling the finished incense in powdered pearl, another lunar materia *par excellence*, the tiny spheres even begin to resemble the full moon herself. If you are planning to work this recipe, please take note of your timing, as you should begin this charm on the evening of the full moon.

Makes: 40–50 incense pearls
Prep time: 1 hour, plus 1 month drying and 3 weeks curing

FOR THE INCENSE
* 28g/1oz frankincense resin
* 5g/0.18oz orris root
* 4g/0.14oz dried mugwort
* 4g/0.14oz dried culinary sage
* Pinch of lotus leaves and stamens (optional)
* Grinding and processing equipment (see page 28)
* Mixing bowl
* Water
* Powdered pearl for rolling (optional)
* Baking parchment/greaseproof/ wax paper
* Airtight jar

1 Gather your ingredients on the evening of the full moon.

2 Finely grind/process all the botanical ingredients to your desired coarseness, but no piece should be larger than a grain of rice.

3 Place these powders in a mixing bowl, and little by little, add water until a smooth, pliable dough forms.

4 Pinch off small amounts of the dough and roll them into pearls about the size of a chickpea/ garbanzo bean. Gently toss the incense in the pearl powder, if using.

5 Set these pearls to dry on baking parchment/greaseproof paper for 1 month. Make sure none of the pearls are touching during the drying process. Transfer to an airtight jar to cure for another 3 weeks.

6 On the following full moon, burn this incense on charcoal to open your full moon ritual or to accompany works of divination, scrying, vision-seeking, and dreamwork.

INCENSE OF THE
GREEN SPIRIT

In modern witchcraft, the terms "natural magic" and "earth-based religion" are used to speak broadly about magic that is rooted in our relationship to the land. Many of these traditions view the witch as set within an environment of spirits, both physical and non-physical, that contribute to the voice of the larger *genius loci*, or spirit of place. Within this spiritual ecology, plants, animals, spirits, and humans all exist in inextricable relationship with this greater *genius loci*. This is true of modern pagan traditions which observe the earth's cycles as part of a sacred progression, and of animistic and indigenous religions which view this spirit as the cause or progenitor of life itself. Communion with the *genius loci* is especially sought where sorcery with inhuman spirits is concerned, such as with plants, animals, and nature spirits, whose consciousness is so different from ours. This loose incense and corresponding ritual are a useful way to experiment with notions of wider spiritual ecologies, and to form a practice around engaging the broader spiritual contexts that we move through every day. Use this recipe as a primary method of forging a relationship with the *genius loci*, or as a new tool to strengthen an existing alliance. The makeup of this incense will be fully yours to create, but ingredient ratios should be followed precisely for best results. Cedar resin is chosen here because of its ubiquity throughout most of the world, but if there are resin-producing trees in your environment, I encourage you to gather and dry your own resin from these.

For this recipe, it is best to select wild plants from wild places, rather than their cultivated cousins in gardens (unless, of course, the garden is your own). Pay particular attention to any plants you already work with in your magical practice, especially those which are aromatic. You can harvest in any season, using any parts of the plants that you like, but take care to harvest enough for your incense, as herbs will lose up to two-thirds of their weight when dried.

Makes: 54g/1.9oz loose incense

Prep time: 20 minutes, plus 3 days drying and 1 month curing

FOR THE INCENSE

* 14g/0.5oz dried herbs from your local environment
* 40g/1.5oz cedar resin
* Grinding and processing tools (see page 28)
* Mixing bowl
* 2 teaspoons rainwater
* Baking parchment/greaseproof/wax paper
* Airtight jar

1 Gather the necessary plants from your environment.

2 Grind/process all the botanical ingredients to your desired coarseness, but no piece should be larger than a grain of rice.

3 Place them in a mixing bowl and mix thoroughly to combine. Add the rainwater and mix, making sure you speak to the plants, asking that they return to you with new life, prepared to be your allies in the work of your craft. Call out to the spirit of the land which resides within each of them, and make your presence and your intentions known.

4 Allow the incense to dry on baking parchment/greaseproof paper for at least 3 days before curing in an airtight jar for 1 month.

5 When the incense is ready, bring it to the most wild, forgotten place you can find and burn the incense there. Accompany this with offerings of fresh water, good bread, or sweet fruits. Speak to the spirit of the land and introduce yourself, stating your intent for the relationship and what you hope to gain. As the incense rises, tell this spirit that each time you burn this incense, you are calling its name, seeking its counsel, and requesting its presence in your work. Use this incense sparingly and mindfully and do your best to ensure that each invocation involves offerings and exchange.

PYTHIA
DIVINATION INCENSE

The Pythia was the famous oracle and prophetess of Ancient Greece. She was situated within the temple of Apollo in Delphi and served as the temple's high priestess. From atop the Pythia's tripod seat, she shared her visions for almost 500 years, beginning at least as early as the 8th century BCE, and came to be regarded as one of the most powerful and reliable seeresses of the ancient world. Her messages, delivered in cryptic poetry from hidden, smoke-filled rooms, are preserved in the writings of the greatest ancient authors, such as Aristotle, Plutarch, Ovid, and Plato.

Despite this long history of acknowledgement, the rituals that allowed the Pythia to prophesize remain largely obscured. However, among the various magical technologies employed within the temple, none is more well-recorded than the use of Apollo's most sacred plant, the bay laurel. The Pythia was said to inhale the vapours of burning bay, and to chew the leaves and seeds of the plant while she worked. Offerings of bay bundles were brought by querents who sought the Pythia's wisdom, and the oracle herself held a branch of these leaves, which rustled and whispered to her as she performed her divinations.

The bay laurel held central importance within the ancient cults of Apollo, with these rites at Delphi being one of hundreds of examples of its use for divination, visions, and the delivery of prophecy.

This recipe may be simple, but it draws on some of the most powerful and well-regarded divination herbs of the ancient world. The olive and the bay are two trees which are said to produce visions of the future, specifically through the burning of their leaves. The blue lotus, more common to Ancient Egypt, also rose to prominence in the ancient world for its delightful fragrance, and its association with producing visions and altered states. In high enough concentrations, the blue lotus can even function as a hypnotic, trance-inducing plant, though this recipe does not employ the lotus' psychoactive nature. Finally, frankincense is an important fragrance used in seeking communion with the spirits who deliver prophecy, especially those who are associated with the sun and the moon – two planetary spheres that are particularly associated with revealing hidden information. For added significance, gather your ingredients on a Sunday at a solar hour, as close to the full moon as possible but not afterwards.

Makes: 40g/1.4oz loose incense
Prep time: 20 minutes, plus 1 month curing

FOR THE INCENSE

* 28g/1oz frankincense resin
* 12g/0.4oz dried bay leaves
* 1 whole blue lotus flower
* Grinding and processing tools (see page 28)
* Mixing bowl
* 1 teaspoon extra virgin olive oil
* Airtight jar

1 Use a spice grinder or pestle and mortar to grind/process all the botanical ingredients to a coarse powder. If you typically prefer a fine powder for your incense, I encourage you to at least leave the bay leaves unpowdered, and in pieces as least as large as grains of rice. This is not a necessary step, and the incense will burn well-powdered or not, but the crackling of these resinous leaves upon hot charcoal was an important aspect of their use in ancient divination practices. These sounds can be listened to by adept scryers for additional information.

2 Place the powders in a mixing bowl. Add the olive oil and stir to combine all ingredients evenly.

3 Transfer the incense to an airtight jar, and cure for 1 month.

4 Burn this incense while performing Tarot readings or other divinations, or before bed to encourage visions in dreams.

HEKATE INCENSE PEARLS

Hekate is a goddess that many witches operating within European traditions will encounter early on in their path. As the patron goddess of two famous mythological witches, Medea and Circe, Hekate is given special reverence by those who practise magic, as she is believed to confer knowledge and magical mastery to her devotees. She is well known for her role in the myth of Persephone, where she guides Demeter's lost daughter home from the underworld, but otherwise Hekate does not feature prominently in the Olympian myths. Instead, much of what we know about this goddess and her rulerships comes from evidence of her thriving cults and her appearance in recorded spells, such as the defixiones or curse tablets of Ancient Greece. While Hekate's attributes have changed and shifted many times throughout the thousands of years of her worship, her patronage of magical people has remained constant.

Many of the ingredients in this blend are important symbols and offerings from Hekate's cults in Ancient Greece. She is often pictured crowned in oak leaves, or described walking between the dreary cypresses of the graveyards. On her monthly feast, the Deipnon, she was offered heads of garlic and raw eggs, which were left at crossroad altars in her honour. As a ruler of the dead, Hekate was frequently worshipped with burning myrrh, an earthy fragrance associated with necromancy in the ancient world. With these associations in mind, this incense is meant to be a suitable offering for Hekate, helpful in making an introduction, or as part of regular new moon rites to the goddess of the witches.

Makes: 40–50 incense pearls
Prep time: 1 hour, plus 1 month drying

FOR THE INCENSE

* 40g/1.4oz myrrh resin
* 6g/0.2oz dried oak leaves
* 12g/0.4oz dried cypress or cedar fronds
* Skins from 3 cloves of garlic
* Grinding and processing tools (see page 28)
* Large mixing bowl
* Pinch of graveyard dirt
* Small mixing bowl
* 1 egg white
* 1 teaspoon water
* Baking parchment/greaseproof/ wax paper

1 Gather your ingredients on the evening of the new moon. Your graveyard dirt can be gathered at any time, but remember to "pay" for this by leaving a coin or small offering in the place from which the dirt is taken.

2 Finely grind/process all the botanical ingredients.

3 Place these powders in a large mixing bowl, along with the graveyard dirt, and mix to combine.

4 In a separate bowl, whisk your egg white with 1 teaspoon of water until it is loose and homogenous. Little by little, add the egg white mixture to your powdered herbs and stir until a soft, smooth dough is formed. If you accidentally add too much liquid, set the bowl on the counter and allow the mixture to dry until it is a workable consistency.

5 Pinch off small amounts of the dough and roll them into pearls about the size of a chickpea/ garbanzo bean.

6 Set these pearls to dry on baking parchment/greaseproof paper for 1 month.

7 On the following new moon, carry this incense to a nearby crossroads and burn it in offering to the Goddess of Witches. Read aloud an invocation of Hekate as the incense burns, such her verse in the Orphic Hymn to the Muses, or one of her many invocations within the Greek Magical Papyri, such as this phonetically pronounced string of barbarous names from the PGM, which is frequently associated with Hekate:

"ASKEI KATASKEI ERON OREON IOR MEGA SAMNYER BAUI PHOBANTIA SEMNE"

AGRIPPA'S VENUS INCENSE

Heinrich Cornelius Agrippa was an author and occult historian who lived in the 15th century. There is much debate about whether he was a practitioner himself, but his greatest work, *Three Books of Occult Philosophy*, details extensive research on astrological concepts, magical plants, mythologies, folkloric beliefs, and magical cosmologies. It is still incredibly useful to magicians today, though many of Agrippa's recipes and anecdotes have not aged well in the 500+ years since its publication. In particular, an oft-cited segment on fumigations for the seven planets gives us a look into the beliefs of early Renaissance magicians, in which animal ingredients and poisonous plants overrun the witch's cabinet. These recipes may sound frightful today, and they are, but they also represent a unique aspect of the European magical current that is worth examining.

Agrippa's original recipe for Venus incense calls for a host of uncommon plant and animal ingredients, including "musk, ambergris, lignum aloes, red roses and red coral" along with "the brain of sparrows and the blood of pigeons". Not only do these ingredients sound impractical, illegal, and difficult to obtain, the fragrance which results from such an incense may not be worth the effort. Especially because the Venusian current in planetary magic is so associated with sweet perfumes and delightful aromas, this medieval recipe raises an important question. What is more important, the ingredients of an incense, or the experience of that incense? Agrippa answers this question himself in the same passage, stating that magical works with benevolent matters, such as love spells, should have a pleasant fragrance, while malefic magical arts, such as cursework, should produce a "stinking fume".

Since I do not share Agrippa's affinity for the smell of burning bird brain, I'd like to propose an alternative, as many others have. My alteration of this recipe is written in keeping with Agrippa's original vision for an incense made from exemplary Venusian ingredients. In my research of European folklore, no plants are more closely associated with Venus than rose, myrtle, orchid, apple, and saffron. These plants occur again and again in charms of love, in dedications to Venusian goddesses, in rites of fertility, and in expressions of romance. Many other plants could be on this list, but I have chosen these five for their ubiquity, accessibility, and the harmony of their fragrances. The resulting incense delights the senses and lifts the spirit, as any true Venusian craft should.

Makes: 40g/1.4g loose incense
Prep time: 20 minutes, plus 3 weeks–1 month curing

FOR THE INCENSE
* 3g/0.11oz dried red rose petals
* 3g/0.11oz dried myrtle
* 3g/0.11oz dried orchid flowers
* 3g/0.11oz dried apple blossoms
* 28g/1oz benzoin resin
* 2g/0.07oz amber resin
* Pinch of saffron (optional)
* Grinding and processing tools (see page 28)
* 1–2 teaspoons neutral carrier oil, such as coconut, avocado, or almond oil
* Mixing bowl
* Airtight jar

1 Grind/process all the botanical ingredients as coarsely or as finely as you like, but let the pieces be no larger than a grain of rice. The benzoin resin should be ground to a similar size, but better results will be seen if it is powdered. You don't need to grind the amber resin, as this is already soft enough to mix into your blend.

2 Place the powders in a mixing bowl and crumble the soft amber resin over the top. Mix to combine, then drizzle with the carrier oil and mix again. The mixture should be loose and crumbly but should leave a firm imprint if a hand is pressed into the herbs. Bakers will know this as a "wet sand" consistency.

3 Place the incense in an airtight jar and cure for 3 weeks to 1 month before use.

4 Burn this incense on charcoal for all works of love, reconciliation, attraction, and conjuring desire.

KYPHI INCENSE PEARLS

Kyphi is a famous Egyptian incense blend with many, many variations throughout history. Popularized by Aleister Crowley at the turn of the 20th century, kyphi rose to prominence in the West amid trends of Egyptian revivalism and popular interest in ancient esotericism. Our earliest references to kyphi are recipes written on Egyptian temple walls from the Ptolemaic period, such as the temple of Horus in Edfu, and Greek texts which date kyphi as far back as 300 BCE. Plutarch tells us that this sumptuous fruit-based incense was burned in Egyptian temples at dusk, just before the shrines were sealed for the day. Each of these sources cites a different variation of the recipe, and many of the original ingredients still have yet to be verified by scholars, so a traditional recipe still eludes us. The recipe in this book draws inspiration from all these sources, focusing on the more accessible ingredients, and omitting those which are hotly debated among scholars, or are very difficult to acquire.

However, it's important to remember that no religion or magical tradition exists in a vacuum.

There is always something to be said of the differences between religion as dogma and religion in practice, and kyphi incense is a perfect example. Throughout its entire history, spanning several thousand years, the Egyptian empire had considerable contact with other nations and cultures. As a colonial nation, Egypt spread its religion far and wide, and these traditions likely saw many unique manifestations among common people as Egyptian magic mixed with local beliefs. Presumably, there were many variants of important recipes such as kyphi, depending upon where the magician operated and what ingredients could be gathered, as attested by the various, disagreeing historical sources we have for this recipe. These variations do not diminish the efficacy of the incense, but simply show aspects of local flavour, cultural exchange, and the personal interpretation of these ancient magicians. In this light, we can choose to see this kyphi recipe here as historically imperfect, or instead, we can view it as but one facet on the brilliant gemstone that is the whole of human engagement with these spiritual mysteries.

Makes: 50–60 incense pearls

Prep time: 1 hour, plus 1 week steeping and 3 weeks drying

FOR THE INCENSE
* 100g/3.5oz/0.5 cup dried sultanas (golden raisins)
* 240ml/9fl oz/1 cup red or white wine
* Airtight jars
* Grinding and processing tools (see page 28)
* 3 tablespoons raw honey
* Small saucepan
* 3 tablespoons frankincense resin
* 3 tablespoons myrrh resin
* 1 tablespoon mastic resin
* 1 tablespoon gum Arabic resin
* 1 tablespoon pine resin
* 2 teaspoons calamus root
* 2 teaspoons spikenard root
* 2 teaspoons juniper berry
* 2 teaspoons dried cassia
* 2 teaspoons dried lemongrass
* Mixing bowl
* Baking parchment/greaseproof/wax paper

1 Steep the sultanas in the wine overnight.

2 Once steeped, seal the mixture in an airtight jar and allow to ferment for 1 full week, making sure to shake daily.

3 When the week has passed, macerate this mixture in a food processor or pestle and mortar until smooth.

4 Stir in the honey, then transfer this mixture to small saucepan. Stir frequently over a low flame until the mixture is reduced by half.

5 While this cooks, finely grind/process all the botanical ingredients.

6 Place these powders in a large mixing bowl and mix to combine.

7 When the wine mixture is fully reduced, stir it into the powders to form a smooth, pliable dough.

8 Once the dough is cool enough to handle, pinch off small amounts and roll them into pearls about the size of a chickpea/garbanzo bean.

9 Set these pearls to dry on baking parchment/greaseproof paper for 3 weeks, evenly spaced so that the pearls do not touch, then cure in an airtight jar for 1 additional month.

10 In keeping with the traditional use of this recipe, burn this incense on charcoal at dusk, as an offering to personal gods or in closing during large ritual operations.

NECROMANCY INCENSE

One of the many magical powers attributed to witches that has followed the archetype from the ancient world to today is the ability to commune with the dead. As liminal beings, existing between worlds, witches are credited with an ability to pierce the veil which separates the land of the living from the land of the dead. We see this unique skill featured prominently in the stories of famous mythological witches, such as the Witch of Endor and the Greek sorceress Circe, as well as court documents and confessions from the European witch trials. In Ancient Greek magic, commanding and coercing spirits of the dead played an important role in casting functional spells, since these shades could carry out supernatural actions outside of the magician's physical limitations. In many traditions all over the world, this ability to speak with the dead is presented with important notions of stewardship for these spirits, where the witch cares for, feeds, and strengthens the ghosts of the dead so that they may be useful allies for magical work.

This necromantic work can embody many aims, and is a useful skill for any practitioner to develop. It has been used in the delivery of divinatory or prophetic information, to seek out and receive ritual instructions from spirits, and even to strengthen the relationships with one's own ancestors and beloved dead. The ingredients in this blend have been carefully chosen for their associations with the dead and, in particular, with causing the dead to speak. There are two optional ingredients presented in this list: styrax resin and grave yarrow. These ingredients may be more challenging to acquire, but have significant historical precedent for their use in necromancy and receiving answers from the dead.

Makes: 45g/1.6oz loose incense

Prep time: 20 minutes, plus 3 weeks curing

FOR THE INCENSE

* 28g/1oz opoponax resin
* 2g/0.07oz black styrax resin (optional)
* 2g/0.07oz dried mullein leaves
* 5g/0.18oz dried cypress or cedar fronds
* 3g/0.11oz sycamore bark or leaves
* 2g/0.07oz dried wormwood
* 1 sprig of yarrow, plucked by the left hand from a graveyard (optional)
* Grinding and processing tools (see page 28)
* Mixing bowl
* 1 teaspoon neutral carrier oil, such as coconut, avocado, or almond oil
* Airtight jar

1 Begin on a Saturday at a Saturnian hour (as Saturn is the planetary ruler of death), though working by the Moon (on a Monday at a lunar hour) would also be acceptable.

2 Grind/process all the botanical ingredients to your desired coarseness.

3 Combine these powders in a mixing bowl, then stir in the oil.

4 Transfer the incense to an airtight jar to cure for 3 weeks before use.

5 Burn in rituals which seek communion with the dead or with one's ancestors, particularly on holidays which are sacred to the dead, such as Halloween, the winter solstice, or at regular rites of veneration for your ancestors.

OFFERING INCENSE STICKS

Spirit work can be very daunting for inexperienced practitioners. Consorting with spirits has been an important aspect of what makes magic work throughout history, but there is lots of incomplete, conflicting information everywhere you look about how to begin this process. Ritual instructions for contacting spirits vary from tradition to tradition, and different cosmologies present contrasting explanations for what spirits are and how they function. Feeling lost in the early stages of your spirit work journey is common. However, there is often an over-emphasis on knowing the "right way" to perform magic, such that many feel paralyzed from action until they have read, researched, and understood "enough". From my years of dedicated study, I can confirm that "enough" knowledge is an elusive, ever-moving threshold, and that practical experience fumbling with magical tools will often reveal a wealth of hidden information that books simply fail to convey. Especially with spirit work, which must be experienced in order to be understood, getting out of the armchair and into the field is one of the most reliable ways to determine what actually works and what doesn't.

Luckily, we are not completely helpless, and have a few simple tools we can use to make an initial foray into the world of spirit contact. Throughout history and across cultures, it has been understood that communion with spirits must be an exchange – that the querent must arrive with a clear agenda for what they hope to gain, and a sense of what they plan to offer in return, creating a sense of reciprocity. In the ancient world, this offering very frequently came in the form of incense, which was believed to be pleasing to the spirits, and could be sent to their immaterial world by virtue of its rising, aromatic vapours. In many cases, this offertory incense was essential to invoking spirits, without which the charm was incomplete.

Obviously there is lots of nuance with this subject, and nothing in magic is truly "all-purpose", but for lack of something more specific, these incense sticks will do just fine to ensure that a friendly greeting is not empty-handed. This blend is made from herbs that are known for increasing magical potency, elevating the psychic senses, and for being generally pleasing to spirits. This is also a useful recipe for testing your skills with crafting incense sticks, which are easy to store and even easier to burn on the go.

Makes: 30–40 incense sticks

Prep time: 1 hour, plus 3 weeks drying and 1 month curing

FOR THE INCENSE
* 1g/0.04oz frankincense resin
* 3g/0.11oz dried mugwort
* 3g/0.11oz hazel leaves
* 3g/0.11oz lemon balm
* 3g/0.11oz yarrow flowers or leaves
* 4g/0.14oz scraped nutmeg
* 5g/0.18 marshmallow root
* 28g/1oz sandalwood powder
* Grinding and processing tools (see page 28)
* Mixing bowl
* Water
* Baking parchment/greaseproof/wax paper
* Bamboo splits
* Airtight Tupperware

1 Finely grind/process all the botanical ingredients. The powders should then be sifted to ensure evenness.

2 Combine all the powders in a mixing bowl, and little by little add water until they form a smooth, pliable dough.

3 On a sheet of baking parchment/greaseproof paper, roll a thin log of dough to a 2mm thickness. Cut this strip of dough to a length that is 2.5cm/1in less than the length of your bamboo splits.

4 Place one split next to the strip of dough, and gently roll the two together, back and forth until the split is fully and evenly encased.

5 Dry these sticks on a sheet of baking parchment/greaseproof paper for at least 3 weeks, then cure for an additional month in a shallow airtight Tupperware that is long enough to hold the sticks.

6 Use this incense in making generalized offerings on a regular basis, while travelling, or for spirits with whom the magician is less intimately acquainted.

Natural Dyes

Natural Dyes

n this chapter on natural dye practices, it's worthwhile to consider the tradition of colourful magical garments in particular. In the Greek Magical Papyri,[i] ritual robes are typically mentioned as being clean and white in colour. This is no surprise within a religious tradition that emphasized purity as a prerequisite for engaging the will of the gods. In the famous *Book of Abramelin*,[ii] the mage is instructed to procure two robes for the operation – one white, and one red and gold. In the Hermetic Order of the Golden Dawn, colourful robes are used to delineate a magical mindset from a mundane perspective, and many colourful forms of ritual dress are found in this school of magic, particularly the Egyptian-inspired Tau robes. Aleister Crowley recorded many iterations of colourful ritual dress in *The Book of the Law*,[iii] particularly the vestments required for performing the Gnostic Mass. In modern neopaganism, colourful robes receive special attention, and are coordinated to various holidays, such as white robes for Yule and green robes for Beltane. We can also think of the ceremonial dress for folk holidays as being a kind of ritual costume, and these are often quite colourful in nature, like the British Jack-in-the-Green of May Day celebrations, or the flower-studded costumes of Slavic winter carnivals which invoke the coming spring in bright pops of botanical colour.

As practitioners of magic, we cease to live in a purely mundane world. Accepting a magical perspective means our worldview becomes fully enchanted, taking on deeper, richer meanings that are alive with connotations, correspondences, rulerships, and spirits. Within this vantage, everything is intentional, and nothing is without purpose, and this gives greater significance to what we may think of as passive plant qualities, such as fragrance, texture, and particularly colour. Summoning colour as a magic ingredient feels like a modern practice, especially in a world where artificially coloured candles, pigmented incenses, dyed crystals, and dazzling glitters are found commonly in occult shops. But although our approaches are modern, the technology of colour magic is very, very ancient, arising from a cosmology that viewed all aspects of material reality – especially colours – as emanations of the divine.

If you've ever practised sympathetic magic, you may already be familiar with this perspective. Within the sympathetic system of magic, when we invoke a colour, we actually call upon a larger archetype of rulerships and correspondences, extending from the lowest lows to the highest highs. These colour correspondences will naturally shift from culture to culture and over time, but colour correspondences for magical work are found all over the world, from the colour-coded chakras and the coloured hues of auric fields to the colours associated with saints and spirits and the shades used in magical symbols like those of each point on a pentagram. This calls us to think of colours as a magic tool, which can be added to our workings as a kind of ingredient, invoked through the compounds and colour-producing chemicals found in plants and minerals.

Sympathetic charms rely upon the idea of shared resonance between two entities, such that they are bound together and can influence one another by virtue of their likeness. For example, if I craft a poppet of a person, which looks like them and may incorporate some of their personal materia like a strand of hair, I can use this representation to act upon them sympathetically. This is also the thought behind many of our notions of magical correspondence, especially within planetary magic. The mechanism that allows us to say that certain herbs or stones are "lunar" or "solar" in nature comes from the Ancient Greek concept of *sympatheia*, literally meaning "fellow-feeling". This concept has a cosmology inherent to it, which describes a living universe in which all of material reality contains intelligence and spirit. This animistic perspective sees this all-pervasive intelligence as originating within the central world-soul, the *anima mundi*, which represents all consciousness within the universe. Ancient Greeks believed this massive and all-containing spirit of the world soul could be broken down into seven energetic currents, named after the seven classical planets. Think about how a Tarot deck represents all aspects of human experience, and yet can be broken down into 78 unique faces – this is similar to how the planetary spheres represent the *anima mundi*. Within this system, each of the seven spheres governs an archetype, an aspect of the world soul, down through which chains of correspondence and causality run between the mundane world and the supermundane spiritual world. If one wants to work magic by the planet Mars, which governs competition and survival, they can select from materia within this current – like thistles, blood-red flowers, or crimson stones like carnelian – to call upon the Martial current by virtue of their shared resonance. Traditionally, these seven spheres are assigned specific cardinal colours as well – gold or yellow for the Sun, silver or white for the Moon, orange for Mercury, green for Venus, red for Mars, blue for Jupiter, and black for Saturn.

Chromamagic has interesting manifestations in occult history, showing us a number of unique applications for colour as a magical ingredient. In ancient magic, we see pigment-producing dye plants appear as herbs of magical enchantments by virtue of their unique colour-producing properties. Many of these magical dye plants, such as saffron, dyer's alkanet, juniper, and safflower, are said to have been favoured by the mythical witch Medea, who received her tutelage in magical herbs directly from the goddess Hekate. It's no secret that colour magic was alive and well in Ancient Greek religion, and was used to make ritual inks and paints for religious statuary that invoked the gods through various shades. This made classical antiquity an incredibly colourful period in history, with even the stark-white marble statuary that we inherit from the Ancient Greeks having been richly painted and coloured in their prime. In contrast, the oppressive Christianity of the late medieval period in Europe saw bright colours as an extension of the Devil's constant temptation, and pious believers cloaked themselves in sombre colours like black and blue to avert his malicious influence. In the early Renaissance, Agrippa writes extensively about colour magic in *Three Books of Occult Philosophy*,[iv] using colour to describe the energetic allegiances between planets, elements, animals, herbs, and crystals. Many magicians and magical writers have produced their own versions of these correspondence lists, including the famous ceremonial magician Aleister Crowley, who includes colour as an important aspect of his rulership charts in *Liber 777*,[v] assigning hues to Tarot cards, astrological signs, and sephirot along the kabbalistic Tree of Life. Colours are also intimately woven into alchemical magic, associated with each step of the alchemical process, to the extent that these transformative stages are referred to by their cardinal colour, such as *citrinitas*, the yellow stage, or *rubedo*, the "reddening" stage. In the last 200 years or so in the West, the emphasis on esoteric colours has been popularized and secularized, removed from |its religious origins in Greek magic to interpret colour as a magic tool all of its own. The famous Order of the Golden Dawn invoked colour magic extensively in their rites, particularly in the polychromatic symbol called the Rosy Cross Lamen, featuring a rainbow blossom at its centre.

In the early 20th century, the Order of the Golden Dawn used colour magic in many of their rites, particularly in the creation of the initiatic Vault, a hypnotically coloured room with seven sides used to "incubate" the adept, specifically by using stark colour contrasts which create a disorienting retinal burn. Contemporary theosophists explored colour theory as magical technology extensively, associating colours with fragrances and musical notes, and even informing early advertising campaigns which used colour to influence a consumer's decisions. Much of this work with colour has been since validated by modern science, which has demonstrated that colours can even have physiological impact, like lowering our blood pressure and causing effects like inducing hunger or excitement.

However, while colours and dyes are mentioned frequently in historical books of magic, very rarely are the plants that generate these bright pigments listed as well. Since this book aims to counter uses of plants rooted in commodification or objectification, harnessing this colour magic in our ritual robes, clothes, and tools will require us to relate to these plants from an animistic perspective. This calls us back to the original perspective of sympathetic magic, where to call upon a colour was to invoke a spirit and a divine intelligence. As you move through the recipes ahead, I challenge you to explore natural dye practices from this allied perspective, as a communion and collaboration with your plant allies toward a deeper, richer magic.

When we work with plant dyes, we are summoning the mysteries of natural pigment and colour. The brilliant hues and shades found in plants are one of the great many allures of the natural world, providing a palette for our gardens, crafts, and charms that innately attracts us. These natural plant colours, made of pigment compounds like carotenoids, flavonoids, betalains, and chlorophylls, are created by plants to perform expressly this purpose, especially when we're talking about the colours of flowers. These colours are expressed to call forth pollinators and enable plant reproduction, issued forth as a subtle form of chemical attraction magic. Many pollinators like bees and butterflies can see wider spectrums of colours than we can, and these pigments scream to them in ultraviolet hues, revealing hidden caches of sweet nectar and pollen. For creatures that cannot speak as we do, these silent forms of chemical communication are the currency of exchange, and with plants, this outreach often begins with colour.

However, as much as these plant colours enchant us, humans have long struggled with extracting these pigments for ourselves. Many are expressed the brightest in their original setting, within the leaves and petals of plants, and will soften, change, mutate, or disappear completely upon attempts at extraction.

Getting "true" colour from these plants, and achieving "colourfastness", or permanence, with these dyes has been an ongoing science since the ancient world. One year's crop of dye plants may yield completely different shades the following year, and environmental factors such as water acidity, the presence of metals and minerals, and even the nature of our fabrics can have a profound effect on the outcome of dye experiments. While the entire breadth of natural dye practices can take years to study and perfect, this chapter aims to provide a useful introduction to this fabulous, polychromatic art, and provides a selection of useful recipes to begin your own experimentation with harnessing plant pigments in your practice.

For a chart on colours, see pages 220–1.

Dye tools

Finally, here is a brief list of necessary equipment that every dyer, experienced or beginner, should consider. These tools will be essential for completing the full dying process, from mordanting to creating a dye bath. It will be absolutely essential to purchase tools which will be only used for dye work and never for other projects, especially cooking, so keep this in mind before investing in new equipment for your budding dye practice.

* **TUBS & BUCKETS** – These will be essential during the mordanting phase for dissolving your mineral salts, transferring fabrics between baths, and soaking your fibres.

* **STOCK POTS** – Large cooking pots that can be set over a flame will be used for mordanting and preparing dye baths. Some recipes call for a stock pot with steamer. If you do not have a steamer, an upturned colander that fits within the pot works well.

* **SPOONS & TONGS** – These will be essential for stirring fabric and removing fibres and bundles from your hot baths.

* **GLOVES & PPE** – For those with sensitive skin or respiratory systems, gloves and face covers will be helpful in minimizing exposure, especially while measuring out easily inhaled powdered salts like alum.

This long list of mordants, modifiers, and tools can certainly sound daunting, and makes natural dye work one of the most equipment-intensive crafts within this book. However, keep in mind that these mordants and modifiers are often used in very small quantities, and are shelf-stable for indefinite periods of time if properly stored. This craft does require significant investment in tools, time, and resources, so consider buying equipment made of easy-to-clean metal, glass, or plastic, which will last a long time, allowing you to get repeated uses for years to come.

How to make natural dyes

The following procedure outlines a simple overview of the dye process from start to finish, pointing out useful tips and techniques along the way. Follow these instructions, alongside those within the recipes ahead, closely for best results when dying your various fabrics.

STEP 1 –
Scour your fabric

When we buy new fabrics at the store, we often take for granted that these are clean and ready for immediate wear. In truth, many of these have been treated with chemical detergents, starches, and deodorizers which need to be removed before beginning the dye process. Even craft fabrics are often treated this way before sale. It's therefore very important to thoroughly clean and "scour" our fabrics before we begin to ensure they are as "virgin" as possible – just natural fibres, and nothing else. For cellulose fibres, washing soda or soda ash is the preferred scouring treatment to remove all unnecessary compounds, while washing protein fibres often calls for a pH-neutral, scent-free detergent like castile soap or Orvus paste.

1. To determine how much scouring solution to use, we will need to weigh our fabric to start with. As a general rule for either cellulose or protein fibres, a 1–2 per cent concentration by weight of scouring solution is preferred, or 1g/½ teaspoon for every 100g/3.5oz of fabric.

2. Add this scouring compound to a stock pot, dissolve it in warm water, then add your fabric and enough water to submerge completely.

3. Place this pot over a medium flame and bring the water temperature up to 80°C/180°F, or just around a gentle simmer.

4. Hold this simmer for 30 minutes, then cut the heat and carefully use tongs to remove the fabric from the liquid.

5. Rinse the fabric until the water runs clear.

STEP 2 –
Mordant your fabric

Next, we move on to the mordanting phase, which is the most important phase of the dye process. Without this step, our colours will simply wash away from our fabric when the dye process is complete. One of the biggest struggles for beginner dyers using natural plants is getting enough pigment to adhere to our fabric. The plants we use for natural dye are chosen because they produce lots of pigment compounds, but this doesn't necessarily mean that those compounds readily adhere to our fabrics. While they may infuse and liberate beautifully into water when creating a dye bath, we need to use chemical binders, called mordants,

to help these compounds adhere to the fibres of our fabric. The word comes from the French *mordre*, meaning "to bite". These binders cause plant pigments to permanently adhere to natural fibres, allowing them to "bite" into the fabric, creating an unbreakable chemical bond that will withstand successive washing and wearing. Without mordants, our fibres may never take on the rich hues we're looking for, or worse, our colours may fade quickly, rending the laborious task of dying our fabric useless.

There are many kinds of mordant that we can use for natural dye, whether we are dying cellulose (plant-based) fibres or protein (animal-based) fibres. For the experiments listed in this book, we will be discussing dying only natural fibres like these, as synthetic fibres made from petroleum derivatives (polyester, nylon, acrylic, etc.) will struggle to accept a natural dye because they are made of thinly spun hydrophobic plastics. Most of the mordants listed here will be made of mineral or metallic salts, which can be purchased online or in hardware shops with relative ease. Don't let these chemical names deter you – with proper care and handling, these compounds are safe to use, and will be washed completely away from our fabrics after the dye process is complete.

* **ALUM** – The most common mordant for natural dye. This mordant is colourless, easy to source, and fairly non-toxic.

* **FERROUS SULFATE** – Iron mordants have been used since the ancient word for their intense colourfastness. However, these mordants often turn colours toward the darker ends of the spectrum. For rich blacks, moody grays, and deep browns, choose this option for your project.

* **SWEETLEAF/ SYMPLOCOS** – This plant has the unique property of naturally accumulating aluminum from its soil, making it an effective plant-based mordant. However, the symplocos plant grows in very threatened ecosystems, so purchasing this plant from sustainable growers is essential to limit our environmental impact.

* **SOY MILK** – This is not technically classed as a mordant, but rather a chemical "binder" instead. Binders help pigments wrap around natural fibres, but do not complete the process of chemically fusing the pigment to the fabric. As such, dyes made with soy milk mordant may fade over time and require more delicate care. However, soy milk has fast become an accessible, affordable option for home dyers, especially for those who are hesitant to work with metallic salts.

* **TANNINS** – Tannins are also binders rather than mordants, but can help many dyers achieve brighter, bolder colours. There are many natural sources of tannin to be found in plants, such as oak balls, myrobalan, sumac, maple, and eucalyptus.

While these compounds may each add their own gentle chemical hues to the finished product, they will ultimately all be assistive in ensuring proper dye adhesion, no matter which mordant you choose. However, savvy dyers may also wish to experiment with colour modifiers, as these can help adjust the finished hue of your dyes, giving the dyer greater control over the outcome. Many natural pigments are greatly affected by simple chemical shifts in environment and pH, and these modifiers can make a big difference in how these pigments are expressed.

* Acidic modifiers turn colours brighter, lighter, and warmer: citric acid, lemon juice, vinegar

* Basic modifiers turn colours darker, cooler, and richer: baking soda, baking powder, wood ash

* Rust liquor, made from rusting iron in a 1:1 solution of vinegar and water, will darken your colours, enriching deep, cool hues and adding brown shades to warm colours.

Professional dyers who work with natural dye on cellulose fibres will often recommend a tannin bath for your fabric before moving on to the mordanting phase, as these compounds help fabric accept a mordant more easily. If you choose to add this optional, additional step for brighter, stronger colours, use powdered tannins like oak gall or myrobalan, and follow directions on your package to see how much to add for your project. However, many dye plants like pomegranate, eucalyptus, yarrow, and avocado stones are rich in natural tannins, making this step redundant. Use your best judgement and experiment with these steps to determine the best procedure for your specific dye and fabric.

Regardless of whether or not you opt for a tannin bath, the mordanting process is absolutely essential. This should be undertaken using damp fibres, as these will absorb mordant liquid more easily, and therefore it is recommended to move into the mordanting phase immediately after scouring.

1 To create a mordant bath, consult the ratios below, given as a percentage of your WOF (weight of fabric). For example, alum is used at 12 per cent WOF, meaning you should use 12g of alum powder for every 100g/3.5oz of fabric.

2 When the mordant bath is prepared, repeat the process you used to scour your fabric. Heat the liquid over a medium flame to around 80°C/180°F or a gentle simmer.

3 Submerge your fabric and simmer for 1 hour, then use tongs to carefully remove the fabric from the mordant bath.

4 Rinse this fabric thoroughly.

This mordant liquid can be used for multiple rounds of fabric, so savvy dyers will make the best use by mordanting several dye projects at once. Note that you can mordant fabric and then save it for use on another day if you are not ready to dye immediately.

Mordant	Percentage Weight of Fabric
Alum	12 per cent
Ferrous sulfate	2–5 per cent
Sweetleaf/symplocos	50 per cent
Soy milk	1:5 soy milk to water

STEP 3 –
Prepare your dye bath

With the hard calculations out of the way, it's time for the fun part of working with natural dye! In creating our dye bath, we get to allow the plants we love to express their beautiful pigments and colours. While previous steps have called us to work with unfamiliar chemicals and precise measurements, preparing your dye bath is as simple in procedure as preparing a cup of tea. Once we extract the pigment compounds from our raw plant material, the hard work of this process is pretty much done!

1 To prepare your own dye bath, fill a stock pot with raw plants and water in a ratio of 2:3. For dried plants, use a ratio of 1:3. You will need to make sure there is enough liquid to cover your fabric, but this pot will reduce and simmer down before we are ready for that.

2 Place the pot over a medium flame and bring to a simmer.

3 Cook the dye plants until your desired colour is reached, though this may require the pot to reduce over the course of a few hours. You may choose to keep small strips of fabric on hand to test the strength of your dye. If you are using any modifiers to adjust the colour of your dye, this is the time to add them, using very small quantities at first until the desired colour is achieved. Remember, you can always add more of any modifier, but you cannot remove it once it has been added to the pot.

4 When the dye has reached the appropriate colour, strain this pot and add your mordanted fabric. If you are not immediately moving from the mordanting stage to the dye pot, make sure your fabric is evenly damp, so that the dye may penetrate more effectively. You can use the spin cycle of your washer or evenly dampen the fabric with water and then wring dry.

5 Allow the fabric to simmer in the dye for at least 1–2 hours, stirring occasionally, until it has absorbed as much colour as possible. Once you no longer see the fabric accepting more colour, cut the heat and use tongs to carefully lift the fabric from the bath.

6 Once cooled, this fabric should be dried completely and cured for one week, before being thoroughly rinsed to remove any excess dye. Projects are then ready for immediate wear.

STEP 4 –
Ecoprint

The recipes ahead also discuss a few different applications for ecoprinting, which is a unique application of natural dye that uses the bodies of whole dye plants themselves. To create an "ecoprint", we place fresh or dried dye plants onto your fabric, and then expose it to water, liquid dye, or steam, in order to release the pigments trapped in our plants. This can be a method of dying our fabric without the need to create large, messy dye baths. This process also leaves beautiful stamp-like impressions on our fabric, capturing the gorgeous shapes and organic details of the plants themselves.

The recipes will have detailed instructions on ecoprinting where it is called for, but as an overview, you may begin this process by:

1   Selecting whole flowers, leaves, and petals for your pattern. Prints on one side of your fabric will bleed through to the opposite side, so do keep this in mind.

2   Lay a sheet of damp mordanted fabric on your workstation, then lay your dye plants over the top in the pattern you'd like to create.

3   Use a hammer or mallet to pound these plants into place, breaking their cell structures and releasing the powerful dye within. Place a sheet of thick, durable plastic over the top of your fabric, as this will help hold the flowers in place while keeping the bleeding of colours to a minimum.

4   Starting from one edge, carefully and tightly roll the fabric, and secure this bundle with an elastic bandage, rubber bands, or twine.

5   With your dye bundle prepared, place it into a steamer at the lowest heat for 30 minutes, allowing the plants to open up and surrender their pigments.

6   When time has elapsed, carefully remove your dye bundle and allow it to cool to room temperature before unbinding.

7   Used botanicals can be picked away and discarded, and the fabric should be allowed to dry completely and cure for at least one week before being washed and dried, ready for wear.

The outline in this chapter will provide a useful structure for getting you started. As you read through the recipes in this chapter, you will no doubt see variants of these techniques used to provide unique outcomes (a mix of dye baths and ecoprinting on the Hand-Dyed Tarot Pouch, for example). Once you master the basics of botanical dyes, you can begin to experiment with these techniques on your own.

HAND-DYED TAROT POUCH

When it comes to plants that lend an added boost in intuitive and psychic matters, the witch can find no better allies than yarrow and mugwort. These two herbs are renowned for their capacity to aid in divination, dreamwork, and in sharpening our second sight, making them witching herbs of the highest order. Using a bundle-and-bath technique, we can extract the green, yellow, and brown hues from these two pigment-rich plants and use them to dye a pouch for our Tarot decks, allowing us to carry our divination tools in a shroud of helpful plant spirits. This pouch can be just as easily used for runes, pendulums, or other divining media, especially those that have been consecrated to the Moon, which governs both yarrow and mugwort in planetary herbalism. For added significance, pick your plants on divination holidays, like Beltane or Midsummer, and perform the dye process under the full moon.

Makes: 1 Tarot pouch

Prep time: 2 hours, plus 1 week drying and curing

FOR THE DYE

* 225g/8oz fresh yarrow flowers (or 115g/4oz dried yarrow flowers)
* Small saucepan
* 1 white Tarot pouch made from natural fibres, prepared with mordant
* A handful of fresh mugwort leaves
* Scrap fabric about the size of your Tarot pouch
* Hammer
* Elastic bandage, twine, or rubber bands

I Prepare your dye bath by adding the yarrow to a saucepan, then cover with enough water to submerge your plants (and later your Tarot pouch) completely.

2 Bring to the boil and simmer for 30 minutes.

3 Remove from the heat and allow to cool completely.

4 While the dye bath is cooling, dampen your mordanted pouch if it wasn't mordanted on the same day as your dye process.

5 Strain out the plants from the dye liquid, then bring back to a gentle simmer.

6 Lay your mugwort leaves on the pouch, leaving at least 5cm/2in of space at the top of your fabric. Place the scrap fabric over top of the pouch and use the hammer to pound your mugwort until it leaves an impression in the fabric. Keeping the scrap fabric tight against the surface of your pouch, roll the pouch tightly into log, then secure with elastic bandage, twine, or rubber bands.

7 Add your bundle of fabric to the dye bath. Simmer for an additional 30 minutes, then remove from the heat again and allow to cool overnight.

8 In the morning, carefully remove the bundle from the dye bath and unravel it. Pick off the mugwort leaves, then allow to dry thoroughly and cure for 1 week before washing.

9 For added colourfastness, allow the pouch to dry in the sun, flipping after 1 hour to sun-treat both sides of the fabric.

PROTECTION SCARF

When it comes to protection magic, Mars reigns supreme. In planetary magic, the red planet is said to rule war, combat, and bloodshed, and, conversely, protection from all these themes. As the planet governing all manner of conflict, Mars has the dual ability of being able to call up danger and just as easily dispel it. While the moon is said to offer protection in the form of motherly guidance, it is Mars who rules all powers of fierce protection, especially the creation of wards and averting magic.

This recipe calls upon ingredients of Mars – aromatic wormwood and the iron for which Mars is known – to give colour to a wearable protection charm. While wormwood dye naturally produces varying shades from yellow to pale green, the presence of iron and walnut as modifiers darkens these shades to a warm olive green, unassuming in its simplicity. If you are looking for more of the green wormwood tones, use fresh herbs for this recipe. This scarf, once consecrated, can be worn about the neck as any protective amulet, encircling the wearer in its virtues. While you are welcome to tailor this charm to your own practice and beliefs, consider reading invocations of Mars over your bubbling dye pot, and perfuming this scarf in Martial vapors like dragons' blood, cinnamon, and basil. As Mars is the planetary ruler of this work, it's best to begin this recipe on a Tuesday in the waning of the moon.

Makes: 1 scarf

Prep time: 2 hours, plus 1 week curing

FOR THE DYE

* 5 rusty iron nails
* 4 whole walnut hulls, dried, or 6 tablespoons crushed walnut hulls
* 180g/2 cups wormwood, fresh or dried
* Stock pot
* 1 plain white cotton scarf, prepared with mordant
* Cheesecloth or sieve/fine-mesh strainer

1 Prepare your dye bath by placing the rusty nails, walnut hulls, and wormwood in a large stock pot, then cover with enough water to submerge them completely.

2 Bring to the boil and simmer for 1 hour.

3 Remove from the heat and allow to cool.

4 While the dye is cooling, if your scarf was not mordanted on the same day as your dye process, gently dampen the fabric with water.

5 Strain out the plants from the dye liquid, then bring back to a gentle simmer.

6 Add the fabric to the pot, stirring gently, and simmer for a further 30 minutes.

7 Turn off the heat and allow the pot to cool completely before removing your fabric. Allow the scarf to hang dry completely and cure for 1 week. Rinse your scarf thoroughly before wearing.

DYING MAGICAL CORDS

Yarn, string, and knot magic come from a humble thread of folk charms that many may not immediately associate with plants. These spells have their origins in the deeply ancient world, with references to knot charms and string magic going back as far as the first human cities. Here, benefic and malefic charms were woven in cords of wild grasses and fragrant cedar bark, healing or cursing the target bound in thread according to the witch's will. In ancient cosmologies, images of gods and goddesses winding the cords of fate abound, and knot magic has famously been used by mortal witches to bind the turnings of the weather and the sea as well. A powerful tool in the hands of the wise, these cords have always been made of simple plant and animal fibres – as humble and domestic an ingredient as we can imagine. But just as the ways of magic are unlocked by the cunning who seek to cultivate relationships with spirits, plants, and the land, so too is this humble magic used to formidable ends when employed in the hands of one who knows its tricks.

To make your own red cords, begin with pre-mordanted yarn of a natural fibre. Since natural yarn, especially wool, has a tendency to pill and felt, make sure to handle your yarn gently, avoiding wring-drying or scrubbing.

As cords are often used in protection and banishing magic, under the rulership of Mars, it may be best to begin this project on a Tuesday in the waning of the moon. However, if you are crafting yarns for a different purpose, choose your timing accordingly.

Makes: 1 skein of yarn (about 100g/3.5oz)
Prep time: 3 hours, plus 1 week drying and curing

FOR THE DYE

* 100g/3.5oz red madder root, ground fine
* 100g/3.5oz red sandalwood, ground fine
* Large stock pot
* A few tablespoons of vinegar (optional)
* Cheesecloth or sieve/fine-mesh strainer
* Yarn or cordage made from 100 per cent natural fibres, prepared with mordant
* Tongs

I Prepare your dye bath by placing the ground madder and sandalwood in a stock pot, then cover with enough water to submerge your plants completely.

2 Bring to the boil and simmer for at least 1 hour. Test the dye to check the shade. If it is too pale, reduce the dye with further simmering. If it is too dark, add a few tablespoons of vinegar to modify the colour.

3 Remove from the heat and allow the dye liquid to cool.

4 Strain out the plants from the dye liquid, then bring back to a gentle simmer.

5 Use water to dampen your yarn, then place in the dye bath, stirring gently to ensure it is fully submerged. Simmer for 1 hour, stirring occasionally, then use tongs to carefully remove from the heat and allow to cool.

6 Air-dry the yarn completely, then allow to cure for 1 week before washing to remove any dye residue. Bind and store the yarn near your home altar, where it can be set aside as a magical tool.

DYED LINENS FOR DREAMWORK

Dream incubation is one of the oldest skills of magic and one of the most ancient forms of divination. The dream state is privileged within witchcraft as a portal to the subtle world of spirts, explorable by the astral or psychic body during sleep. Ancient Mesopotamian witches would bathe in starlit waters to conjure cunning dreams, and medieval Europeans would fashion flower crowns of sacred blooms to wear to bed in the hopes of dreaming truth about their future. While pillow charms, bed-blessing spells, and sleeping talismans abound in history, there are few sources for linens, nightgowns, or materia magica set apart for dreamwork. This recipe is my answer to the modern witch's dream incubation ritual, elevating every aspect of our sleep routines. Using two important lunar plants of dreamwork – elder and juniper – this set of consecrated dream linens (one sheet, one fitted sheet, and two pillowcases) invites us to consider all aspects of our lives as spaces for magic, no matter how ordinary.

For added significance, as this work is consecrated under the moon, it is best to begin on a Monday, as near to the full moon as possible, but not afterwards.

Makes: 1 set of linens

Prep time: 1 hour 30 minutes, plus 1 week curing

FOR THE DYE

* 135g (about 1.5 cups) dried juniper berries
* 170g (about 1.5 cups) dried elderberries
* 4 tablespoons warm water
* 1 set of 100 per cent cotton linens, prepared with mordant
* Elastic bandage, twine, or rubber bands
* 1.5l/52fl oz/6 cups water
* Large stock pot with steamer

1 Rehydrate the dried berries by soaking them in a few tablespoons of warm water. Let them stand, covered, for 1 hour.

2 When the berries are ready, clear a large, flat workspace. Dampen your mordanted fabric if it wasn't mordanted on the same day as your dye process, then lay it flat on your workstation. If space is tight, ensure there is room for at least half the sheet. Scatter some of your berries across one half of the sheet, ensuring that you have enough berries saved for the pillowcases and fitted sheet. Fold the other half of the sheet over the first, with the berries sandwiched in between.

3 Starting from the narrow end, carefully roll the sheet up as tightly as possible, then roll this fabric log into a spiral and secure with elastic bandage, twine, or rubber bands.

4 Repeat this process for the pillowcases and fitted sheet.

5 Bring at least 1.5l/52fl oz/6 cups of water to a simmer in your stock pot, then load your linens into the steamer basket. Steam the linens for 1 hour, covered.

6 Turn off the heat and allow the linens to cool in the pot. When cooled, remove the linens, unbind them, discarding the used berries, then allow all linens to dry completely and cure for 1 week. Rinse thoroughly before use.

SPRING EQUINOX RITUAL TABLECLOTH

The spring equinox is an important time for plants in the northern hemisphere as it slowly warms and lightens. The equinox signals a dramatic return of plants to the environment, issuing the death knell for the long, cold winter and the return of colour and fragrance to the landscape, which erupts with pinks, yellows, blues, purples, and greens. It is not just the plants that are celebrated at this time, but the waters of spring as well, which enable this flush of flowers upon the land. For these reasons and so many more, the spring equinox holds a sacred place within the magical calendar, especially where plant magic is concerned.

This cloth is the perfect companion to equinox feasts and rituals. Use as a picnic blanket for your first sacred outdoor meal of the spring. Since this tablecloth represents a snapshot of plant life at a particular time of year, use it as a meditation blanket for communing with the spirits of the season.

To make your own tablecloth, rise early on the spring equinox, preferably when the plants are still sprinkled with morning dew. Gather your dye herbs and leave an offering for the earth in return for your harvest. Ferry your plants home, and trim away any stems or leaves that will not be used in the dye process.

Makes: 1 tablecloth

Prep time: 1 hour, plus 1 week drying and curing

FOR THE DYE

* 1 large white tablecloth made of natural fibres, prepared with mordant
* 900g/2lb fresh spring dye flowers, like dandelion, saffron crocuses, iris, woad, yarrow, ivy, violets, daffodils, peony petals, hyacinth, or others that grow in your region
* Hammer
* Elastic bandage, twine, or rubber bands
* Large stock pot with steamer
* 500ml/17fl oz/2 cups water
* 500ml/17fl oz/2 cups spring rainwater

1 Dampen your mordanted tablecloth and lay it out on a large, flat workspace. Place your flowers on one half of the tablecloth, then fold the other half over the top, sandwiching the flowers between the two sides of the fabric. Use a hammer to tap the flowers, causing them to release their pigment and make firm prints.

2 Starting from a narrow side of the tablecloth, carefully roll the fabric up as tightly as possible, then roll this log into a spiral and secure with elastic bandage, twine, or rubber bands.

3 Fill your stock pot with the water and rainwater, bring to a simmer, then load your tablecloth into the steamer basket. Steam the linens for 30 minutes, covered.

4 Turn off the heat and allow the fabric to cool in the pot. When cooled, remove and unbind the tablecloth, discarding the used flowers and herbs.

5 Air-dry this tablecloth fully, then cure for 1 week before rinsing.

MY OWN ALTAR CLOTH

This is the very cloth which adorns my home altar, upon which all my best magic blossoms. It was hand-dyed in 2020 using plants that are known for their vision-giving properties, and is meant to be a tool of divine inspiration called forth through the plants. The yarrow, elderberry, clary sage and cedar – all traditional plants of divination and second sight – are encouraged to release their pigments in a deep-red dye bath made from pomegranate, the fruit of psychopomps and seers, deepened with dye-rich pokeberry. When my altar is not in use, this cloth is tucked away in a drawer, safe from spills, tears, dust, and the wandering footprints of my cats. But when the full moon rises and it's time for magical work to begin, I tidy my altar and spread this silk across its surface, allowing these plants to be the foundation for my craft, and carrying out my witch-work within their presence.

This altar cloth only exists as an extension of my own practice, born of my beliefs and my deep relationships with all the plants involved. These plants are also emblematic of the land I live on, tied intimately to my physical and spiritual sense of place. You are more than welcome to experiment with the plants listed in this recipe so they represent your sense of place. However, I encourage you to interrogate your own practice, and the wild plants of your own bioregion, seeking botanical allies that might be a better fit for your practice. Since the purpose of an altar cloth is to help us create a proper ritual environment, consider what energies or currents would most assist in your practice. Which plants that grow near you can help you accomplish these goals? Which of these plants are your closest magical allies, or which plants do you already have a relationship with? These questions will help guide you to selecting plants that are meaningful to your own practice and beliefs, yielding a finished product that lends meaningful assistance to your craft.

Makes: 1 altar cloth

Prep time: 2 hours, plus 1 week drying and curing

FOR THE DYE

* Skins of 9 pomegranates
* 700ml/24fl oz/3 cups pomegranate juice
* 120g/0.5 cups fresh pokeberries or blackberries
* Large stock pot
* 1 silk or mulberry silk altar cloth, prepared with mordant
* A few handfuls of fresh rose petals
* A few fresh yarrow flowers
* Handful of fresh elderberries
* A few clary sage leaves
* A few cedar fronds
* Hammer
* Elastic bandage, twine, or rubber bands
* Tongs

1 Prepare your dye bath by placing the pomegranate skins, pomegranate juice, and pokeberries or blackberries in a large stock pot, then cover with enough water to submerge your plants completely.

2 Bring to the boil and simmer for 1 hour.

3 Remove from the heat and allow to cool completely.

4 While the dye bath is cooling, dampen your mordanted silk fabric if it wasn't mordanted on the same day as your dye process, then lay this silk flat on a clean workspace.

5 Strain out the plants from the dye liquid, then bring back to a gentle simmer.

6 Lay your botanicals on half the fabric, working in whatever pattern you wish. Carefully fold the other half of the silk over your plants, encasing them completely in cloth. Press firmly to remove any air pockets and use a hammer to gently pound each leaf and flower until they begin to release a bit of their dye.

Working from one narrow end, carefully roll the silk as tightly as possible, then roll this fabric log into a spiral and secure with elastic bandage, twine, or rubber bands.

7 Place your bundled silk in the dye bath and simmer for 30 minutes, stirring occasionally. Turn off the heat and use tongs to carefully remove the silk from the pot. Unbind the fabric, discard the used plants, then allow the silk to dry completely and cure for 1 week before washing.

ECO-PRINTED
RITUAL GOWN

A magician's gown is the high glamour of magic rites, and a method of cloaking ourselves in our sacred pigments and plant allies to allow a proper ritual state of being. This dress will probably be the most complex natural dye project in this chapter because we will work to dye both the front and back of this dress, creating a garment that appears to be growing over with plants. This method has been made as simple as possible, by using the bath of plant material to print on both sides of the dress. Carefully follow the directions below for best results, but don't be too intimidated by the process. If medieval dyers with limited equipment could make beautiful ecoprint designs, so can you!

This dress is meant to represent the wearer, enrobed in an expression of their magical practice. As you design your own gown, consider how you might represent your practice through this medium. I encourage you to reach for the plants that serve as your closest botanical allies, and craft your design with intention and abandon, making this project a vibrant expression of your true will.

Makes: 1 gown
Prep time: 1 hour, plus 1 week drying and curing

FOR THE DYE
* 1 white dress made of natural fibres, prepared with mordant
* Selection of plant material for printing
* Plastic garment bag or other plastic barrier sheet, enough plastic to cover the front, back, and interior of the garment completely, with 3 large sheets of plastic in total
* Hammer
* Elastic bandage, twine, or rubber bands
* Large pot with steamer

I Choose a workspace that will allow you to spread your fabric out completely. A large dinner table is perfect, but a clean floor works just as well.

2 Dampen your mordanted fabric if it wasn't mordanted on the same day as your dye process, then turn the dress inside out and lay it out as flat as possible on your workspace.

3 Begin laying your plants between the two layers of fabric, on what is now the "inside" of your dress. When the dress is turned right-side-out after steaming, the prints will show symmetrically on the front and back of the dress. When you have completed your design, use the hammer to gently tap them, so they release their pigment compounds.

4 Starting along the bottom of your dress, carefully roll the fabric up as tightly as possible. Use lots of pressure to hold the plants in place with each twist. When the bundle is fully wrapped, wind the log of fabric into a spiral and secure with elastic bandage, twine, or rubber bands.

5 Fill your pot with 5cm/2in of water, bring to a simmer, then load your tablecloth into the steamer basket. Steam for 15–20 minutes, covered, or until the plants have yielded their colour.

6 Turn off the heat and allow the dress to cool in the pot until it can be safely handled. Once cooled, unroll your bundle and carefully remove the flowers from your fabric. Allow the dress to air-dry completely, then cure for 1 week.

7 Run the dress through a gentle wash and it will be ready for wear.

DRAWING & PAINTING WITH NATURAL DYES

Throughout most of this chapter, our focus has been on properly mordanting our fabric. We've used these compounds and mineral salts to help colour bind to the fibres of our projects, enabling our colour to stay put through successive washes and wears. Now that we've mastered the chemistry of mordanting, I'd like to explore using mordants and fixatives in a new way, to help us achieve crisp patterns and hand-painted designs on our fabrics. This is perfect for painting sigils and symbols onto ritual clothing and altar cloths, or creating your own patterned fabrics for any project you choose.

This recipe is a fantastic way to utilize leftover dye after completing another project. Since dye baths are not shelf-stable, consider freezing leftover dye liquid to use for projects like this one, which only require a few tablespoons of concentrated dye liquid to complete.

Makes: a few tablespoons of paintable dye
Prep time: 20 minutes, plus 1 week drying and curing

FOR THE DYE

* Any plain colourless cloth made from natural fibres, prepared with mordant and fully dried
* A few tablespoons of leftover natural dye
* 1 tablespoon cornflour/cornstarch or guar gum
* Paintbrush, stamps, or stencils
* Stock pot

1 Make sure your cloth is fully dried after mordanting to ensure crisp edges on your patterns.

2 Mix a small quantity of leftover dye (only as much as you plan to use) with your cornflour or guar gum, stirring well to ensure no lumps remain. You can thin the mixture with more dye if it becomes too thick; you want it to have a gel consistency similar to ketchup or mustard.

3 Using a paintbrush, stamp, or stencil, thinly paint designs of your choosing upon the fabric. This dye will soak through your fabric, so plan to have designs show on both sides. Try not to oversaturate the fabric, as your dye could bleed.

4 When finished, allow the project to dry completely, then cure in a cool, dry place for at least 1 week.

5 When your fabric has cured, gently run it under cold water to rinse away any extra dye and thickening agent, then wash the fabric on the delicate cycle of your washer.

6 Allow the material to dry in the sun to improve your colourfastness, flipping after 1 hour.

Inks

Inks

When we use inks within a magical context, two different techniques are employed. First, as we discussed in our chapter on Natural Dyes, the use of chromamagic, or colour as a magical ingredient, gives us a symbolic method for invoking spirits and energies through the spectrum of visible light. The use of coloured inks in textual magic extends as far back as Ancient Egypt, where spiritual documents were inscribed in bold red cinnabar inks, called "snake blood", to delineate their separation from mundane transcriptions. At the same time, when these pigments are used in writing, we perform a kind of binding charm that fixes our works and intentions in the external world. We will revisit this technique again in the textual and figurative spells discussed in the Paper chapter (see pages 112–15), where inscribing a symbol or sacred name can be used to consecrate a talisman, or create a sigil to actualize our goals. The rich hues of inks and paints are intended for this kind of work, meant to inscribe images and glyphs that are bold and long-lasting. In fact, striving for permanence in ink has long been the work of expert ink makers, ensuring that the marks made by their pigments will outlive and outlast their creators. These marks then become an intergenerational exchange, a necromantic missive between the living and the dead, bridging the past and the future through the sharing of information.

But hunting for permanence or "indelibility" in inks is not an easy task. Natural pigments, once extracted and diluted, often lose their boldness and intensity, and become susceptible to degradation by moisture, sunlight, and the passage of time. Early alchemists struggled to make their herb- and mineral-based inks last, and sought to chemically bind inks to their pages with tannins, resins, and metallic salts. One of the most famous European ink recipes, which held dominance from classical antiquity until the invention of the printing press, was made from tannin-rich oak galls and ferrous sulphate, called copperas or vitriol. This recipe is too toxic to include in this chapter; oak gall inks were so strong that, if improperly diluted, they could burn right through a page. Because of their extreme permanence, we see gall nut inks cited in texts that involve pacts with spirits, especially the Devil, as one 14th-century notation suggests. These gall inks were also mentioned in ancient spellbooks like the *Greek Magical Papyri*, where one recipe (PGM 12) uses sacred figures inscribed in gall nut ink on wormwood roots to produce a talisman for winning love, friendship, and the admiration of all. This specific recipe also includes the aromatic myrrh resin, mentioned in many magical ink formulas from this time period, which acts as a natural fixative and binder, further ensuring the ink's fidelity.

While it has certainly faded from prominence in the modern occult, the crafting of magical inks has a long and beautiful history. Many of these recipes are highly specialized, calling on not just bold mineral pigments like ochre and cinnabar, but specific plants as well. One additional recipe from late antiquity (PGM 1) detailed an ink made from myrrh, pinecones, figs, ibis wings, dates, and the famous "single-stemmed wormwood" cited frequently in magical charms. This ink is meant to be used to inscribe a long list of sacred names, before being washed away from the papyrus and drunk by the magician, who literally takes the fixed words of the charm into their body. In the *Long Lost Friend*,[vi] a book of Pennsylvania Deutsch magic, a magician is cited as using magical red ink to copy lines from the *Seventh Book of Moses*,[vii] and using them to make a pillow charm for healing sickness in a young baby. In the famous *Key of Solomon*, rituals are given for consecrating both the ink and inkwell of the magician, and formulas are included for crafting magical inks used to draw the symbols of the pentacles, including recipes which use the blood of animals, like crows and bats, as their primary ingredient. These blood inks feature heavily in the grimoires of the Middle Ages, for spells ranging from protecting one's garden to invoking the planetary spheres. In the *Picatrix*,[viii] a book of astrological magic from the 11th century, specific recipes are given for inks under the rulership of the twelve zodiac signs, occurring in a variety of hues and shades. Ink was also used as a scrying media in Ancient Babylon and Egypt, where young boys stared into black pools of ink held in their cupped hands in order to see visions of the gods. In all these manifestations of ink magic, it is the power of ink to bind our words in permanence and make lasting symbols of our will that is called upon as a magical quality.

It's important to remember that ink has broader artistic applications than just as a writing medium. Art is a significant aspect of magical craft, as both practices rely upon a command of the generative, creative channel of the psyche to make our will manifest in the world around us. In figurative charms,

which deal with drawing figures or symbols to create paper talismans, magical inks are often mentioned in tandem. These charms become a dance between ink, paper, and symbol, requiring all three aspects to be of the right condition for the charm to be effective. This technology features heavily in religious iconography, which associates the depictions of spirits with specific colours, such as how the Virgin Mary is always cloaked in a specific shade of blue, called "Marian blue", to denote her piety and virginity. Using these magical tools and techniques as artists allows us to tap into deeper levels of significance and intentionality in our creations, perhaps fashioning paintings, drawings, and art pieces which are spells themselves. These art-charms follow in the tradition of artist-magicians throughout history, like Austin Osman Spare, Kenneth Anger, Hilma af Klint, Remedios Varo, and more.

The recipes that follow in this chapter prepare you to explore the transformative power of magical inks using a variety of media. These examples are written to be infinitely customizable, able to be tailored to your specific intent just like the magic inks of history. While some mineral inks are present, like "snake blood" tempera paint and traditional lampblack, most of these recipes are fully plant-based, requiring only a few simple ingredients to prepare. These formulas will encourage you to scour your local environment for magical pigments, and lean into your creative side as you draw talismans, charms, and magical artworks with your new homemade inks and paints.

Ink tools

Like most of the crafts in this book, inks can be made easily at home using tools you likely already have. While the recipes ahead will differ in their formula and approach, there are a few important tools you may want to have before beginning your ink-making journey:

* **SIMMERING VESSELS** – Many inks require a steep in hot water in order to bring out botanical colours. Especially if you're working with poisonous or toxic dye plants, it's important to have separate pots and pans for your ink making to the ones you use for cooking. For ink recipes, a small saucepan (that holds around 1 litre/1 quart of liquid) is typically sufficient.

* **STRAINING TOOLS** – Depending upon the plants you use in your blend, a strainer may be needed to remove organic material from your final inks. Muslins, sieves/fine-mesh strainers, and coffee filters are all good choices.

* **AIRTIGHT STORAGE VESSELS** – Once your ink is made, you will need to store it in a way that limits contact with outside bacteria and prevents evaporation. Airtight vessels, like Mason jars, are great for this craft.

How to make inks

The ink-making process opens us up to a fabulous tableau of rich botanical colours. Just as with the process of extracting natural dye, making ink requires us to seek out and isolate powerful plant pigments. While dyes require complex mordanting processes and elaborate set-ups to perform pigment extractions, the ink-making process is relatively simple, and can be accomplished with a few bowls, spoons, a small pot, and a hob/stovetop. In some cases, heat may not even be necessary to complete the pigment extraction. For those seeking to explore the bold natural palette of the plant

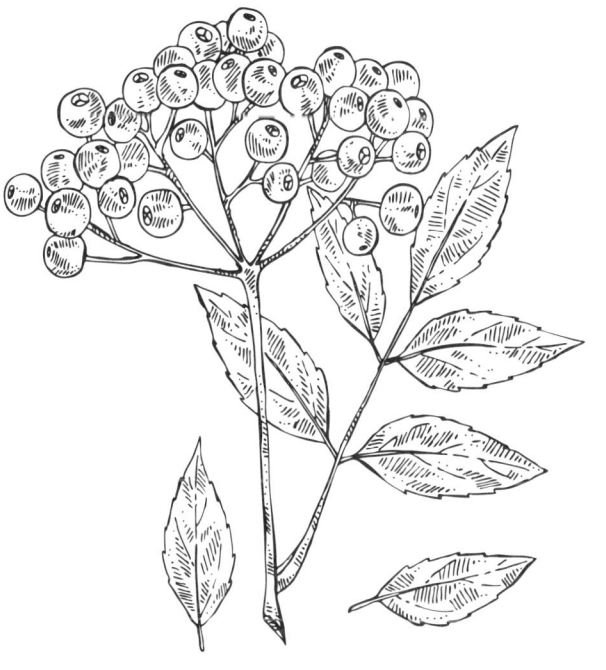

kingdom, especially artists and illustrators, the process of making inks and paints at home can be simple to pick up, and incredibly rewarding.

The recipes ahead will introduce a number of ink-making methods, from water and alcohol extractions, to mineral-based pigments, to quick recipes for turning foraged flowers into natural inks. While each of these procedures has unique steps meant to introduce you to a variety of ink-making techniques, there are some useful notes about the ingredients required that may be helpful to share before your experiments begin. While the ingredients of each recipe will have their own nuance and specific chemistry that require individual approaches, most recipes will contain at least four ingredients: a pigment source, a solvent, a binder, and a preservative. Being able to identify and wield these ingredients will enable plenty of customization and experimentation, allowing you to create recipes of you own once you master a few basic techniques.

STEP 1 –
Choose your ink pigments

In our chapter on Natural Dyes, we introduced the botanical origins of plant pigments, and the compounds that contain the most organic plant colour. However, the pigments of the dye process are often gentler and weaker than those required for ink making, which necessitates a bold stoke that will be visible upon a page. While dye processes can be successful in yielding soft tones and gentle shades, our inks need to be bold if they are to be legible in writing. For this reason, plant pigments are often simmered for longer times in smaller batches of liquid to attain a stronger colour. Many inks even rely on pronounced mineral pigments, like cinnabar and lampblack, because they produce such beautifully intense colours.

In selecting plants for the ink-making process, try to choose those that contain bolder, darker hues, especially if your intention is to use them for writing or drawing sigils. For art inks, such as those used for painting and drawing, softer shades can be attained by diluting our inks, either in a palette or on the page, similar to the way in which watercolour paints are used. Knowing that we can always dilute for softer shades, it benefits the practitioner to create stronger "mother" inks, which are rich and bold, and can be softened and blended to achieve an entire range of shades and tones. However, because inks are also used in small quantities and can often have a shorter shelf life, it's recommended to create batches that are relatively small, perhaps a cup of ink at most.

STEP 2 –
Add solvent

In order for our plant pigments to be useable by a pen, brush, or quill, we need to liberate them in a liquid solvent. This liquid is often simply water, as many of the pigment compounds we'll be seeking out are water-soluble, and only require a quick infusion over a warm flame in order to be extracted. This process is as simple as making a pot of tea, and as long as our plant material is ground or chopped finely and allowed to steep for long enough, a water extraction is typically sufficient for creating bold plant-based inks. However, in extracting from plant materia that is hydrophobic, such as resins like dragon's blood and myrrh, an alcohol solvent may be preferable. These alcohol-based inks have the benefit of being more shelf-stable, but can also quickly evaporate if stored incorrectly. Alcohol inks will often generally be thinner in consistency, as common binders like acacia powder are not alcohol-soluble but may have their own natural thickeners, as alcohol does not just extract from plant resins, but often liquifies them entirely.

STEP 3 –
Add binders

When we think about the difference between inks and paints, it's often all about consistency. Inks are typically liquid throughout, while paints tend to have a gel texture. This all comes down to the types and quantities of binders used, which can create pigments that are translucent or opaque, and as thin or thick as we need them to be. Most of the recipes in this book rely upon the most common ink binder that has been used since the ancient world, which is powdered gum Arabic, from the acacia tree. This non-toxic natural resin

is fully soluble in water, and will help thicken our inks enough to be held by brushes or ink pens, without making them opaque or changing the colour. Ideally, we should add enough binder so that the ink is as viscous as double/heavy cream.

One recipe in the chapter ahead, Snake Blood Ink, uses a simple technique for homemade tempera paint, using egg yolk as a binder. However, egg yolks have their own colour and opacity, and this is something to keep in mind if you choose to experiment with making more tempera paints at home, since this will necessarily affect your final product.

STEP 4 –
Add preservatives

As mentioned previously, alcohol-based inks do not require a preservative. These pigmented tinctures are as shelf-stable as a bottle of vodka, and can last for years if stored in airtight vessels that prevent evaporation. However, water-based inks do not have these natural preservative qualities, and require additional plants or compounds to help stave off mould and bacteria. In the Middle Ages, small bottles of ink could be preserved by adding a few whole cloves, which gently infuse the ink with their natural antimicrobial properties. Wintergreen extract is also a favourite among ink makers, though other antimicrobial extracts and essential oils could just as easily be used here, like rosemary, oregano, or tea tree. When all else fails, small quantities of vinegar or alcohol (at least 20 per cent of your final blend) can serve as natural preservatives as well, though it's important to keep in mind that vinegar is a colour modifier, and may turn your inks toward the warmer, brighter side of the colour spectrum. If this is not your preference, use alcohol instead.

Additionally, the work of preserving water-based inks extends beyond simply adding preservative plants and extracts. Making sure to use clean jars and tools, as you would in canning jams and jellies, can help prevent unnecessary introductions of mould and microbes to your ink. Once contamination is spotted, the ink can become toxic to use and must be thrown away, so it's best to prevent all avenues of transmission if possible.

As you work through the recipes ahead, take note of the variance between them, and how each ink formula uses these four basic ingredients to capture plant pigments in unique ways. There are numerous experiments in this chapter, as well as recipes that invite your own customization, allowing you to tailor your inks to the plants that grow in your own environment. As you use these homemade inks in your practice, for writing sigils, inscribing your personal grimoire, or creating magical artworks, the imprint of these plants and honoured allies, as well as the wider spirits of your local ecology, will shine through.

INVISIBLE INK

You may already have some experience making invisible inks as a childhood craft. Using lemon juice and heat, as seen in mystery movies and novels, we can conceal or reveal our hidden writings at will, in a flourish of chemistry that looks like magic to the untrained eye. The desire for sending hidden messages is recorded extensively within the ancient world, using codes and hidden letter compartments to deliver clandestine correspondence. The first recorded use of invisible ink dates to the 3rd century BCE, a clear ink made from tannin-rich nut galls, which became visible when treated with metallic salts.

These invisible inks are often called "sympathetic inks", because they operate within two parts: one clear-drying liquid to inscribe the hidden message and one liquid chemical indicator used to reveal it. The chemical reaction between these two compounds is what makes the secret writing visible; they are two sides of the same operation. The use of the word "sympathy" here refers to the Greek concept of *sympatheia* – that certain materials are energetically related to one another by way of a likeness or correspondence, such as the relationships between plants and the planets within Ancient Greek magic and cosmology. To craft your own invisible ink, you will need to prepare your own sympathetic magical reaction from two different mixtures. In this recipe, we'll be using a baking soda mixture as the invisible ink (or sympathetic ink) and grape juice as the chemical indicator.

Makes: about 60ml/¼ cup ink
Prep time: 10 minutes

FOR THE INK
* 2 small bowls
* ½ teaspoon baking soda
* 2 tablespoons water
* 2 tablespoons red grape juice
* Paintbrush
* Paper

I In a small bowl, stir the baking soda and water together until the baking soda has dissolved.

2 Add the grape juice to a second bowl.

3 Using a paintbrush, write your messages using the baking soda solution, which will be visible on the page for just a few seconds before drying. When dry, the writing should be fully invisible. It is important to allow the page to dry fully before proceeding.

4 When you wish to reveal the hidden message, use a clean paintbrush to push the grape juice around the page in broad strokes. As the juice encounters the baking soda, its colour will change from light red to a deep, dark purple.

5 For future use, you can store your baking soda solution in a small airtight ink vial, but the grape juice won't store for long. This ink will be imperceptibly invisible until it encounters a reagent, so unless you reveal the placement and chemistry of your hidden writing to others, your secrets will be completely safe!

LAMPBLACK INK

Lampblank is one of the most famous ink recipes in human history, and for good reason. This potent, permanent black ink, sometimes called India ink, has enabled scribes, artists, and writers to create works that withstand the test of time, without fading or burning through the delicate paper of their documents. This ink is relatively simple to make, using only two ingredients at its core: water and lampblack, or soot collected from burning candles and open flames. It is an effort in fixing the blackening properties of fire into a useable ink, born alchemically from the destruction of plant materia. From the ashes of burnt allies, something new is created within the lampblack, retaining in a certain sense the properties of those plants used in its creation, but in a newly transformed, unrecognizable fashion.

Resinous woods like pine or cedar will produce lampblack readily and effectively, while cleaner burning sources like candles will take longer to produce a suitable layer of soot. You may marvel at how little powder you've actually collected, but remember that historical ink makers would perform this process on massive metal vessels suspended over bonfires, allowing them to collect far more lampblack at once. Luckily, lampblack powder is so potent that only a small amount is necessary to make useable ink. This recipe can be quite time-consuming, but the crafting process can be stopped and restarted at any point.

Makes: 1 teaspoon of ink
Prep time: 1 hour–1 hour 30 minutes

FOR THE INK
* Clean metal or ceramic cup
* Candle, or short length of pine or cedar wood
* Baking parchment
* Paintbrush
* ½ teaspoon water
* Powdered gum Arabic
* Whole cloves

I Start by gathering your lampblack. Suspend your metal or ceramic cup over the flame of a burning candle or small length of burning wood. As the flame tickles the bottom of the cup, you will notice black soot collecting on the outside of the vessel. This is your lampblack powder. When the entire surface of the cup is covered in black powder, extinguish the flame.

2 Working over a sheet of parchment paper, use a dry paintbrush to carefully scrape the lampblack powder off your cup.

3 Repeat the process if necessary until you have collected at least ½ a teaspoon of pure lampblack powder.

4 Mix the lampblack powder with ½ a teaspoon of water, adding more if the liquid is too thick. If you need to thicken the liquid, add small quantities of powdered gum Arabic until the ink is the consistency of double/heavy cream.

5 Pour this ink into an airtight ink vessel, then add a few whole cloves as a natural preservative. This ink can be used immediately.

SNAKE BLOOD INK

The Greek Magical Papyri, or PGM, is a grimoire that contains hundreds of recipes for magical craft, including many ritual inks. One such recipe calls for an ingredient named "haima drakonteion", literally "snake blood", used in the PGM to write the sacred names that conjure spirits of the dead. It's an open secret that, while many recipes call for animal ingredients, these are often code words used by ancient magicians to conceal the true formulae of their recipes. The "snake blood" in this recipe is likely not blood at all, but rather a plant or mineral with a deep red pigment. However, the translation is hotly debated among scholars, with disagreements about which plant was actually the "haima drakonteion" of antiquity. Aside from the common interpretation that it is red resin from the dragon's blood plant (see page 100 for another recipe using this plant), one of the prominent theories points to cinnabar, a bright-red mineral pigment used in paint and ink making, as a likely candidate for the elusive "snake blood" ink of ancient magicians.

Red cinnabar pigment can be purchased online or in art supply shops, but it is important to handle this powder carefully. Natural cinnabar is made from powdered mercury sulfide, which can be toxic if inhaled. For this reason, it's important to set up a proper workstation to avoid spills, and to craft this ink with gloves and a mask. While this may sound daunting to modern witches, practitioners and artists of the past often used these powerful pigments, learning the ways of the earth through careful, respectful approach and study of the mineral's natural toxins. When the properties of a plant or mineral are understood, there is no reason to fear them. With proper precautions, this ancient pigment can still be worked today to produce a fabulous red ink, and provides modern witches with a useful exercise in creating bold, colourful tempera paints.

I strongly recommended you use disposable tools (spoons, bowls, etc.) for this recipe, to avoid any risk of cross-contamination with other projects.

Makes: about 1 teaspoon of tempera paint
Prep time: 10 minutes

FOR THE INK
* 1 teaspoon powdered "snake blood" (red cinnabar) pigment
* Disposable mixing bowl and spoon
* 1 egg
* 5 tablespoons water
* ¼ teaspoon vinegar
* Face mask and gloves

1 Add your red cinnabar pigment to a bowl and use the back of a spoon to press into the powder, ensuring no lumps are present.

2 Gently separate the egg yolk from the white. Carefully tear the yolk sac and empty it into a separate bowl. Add the water and vinegar and stir until evenly mixed.

3 In keeping with the ancient origin of this ink, this recipe uses a traditional formula for basic egg tempera. Tempera paints hold colour impressively well but dry very quickly, so you should make only as much paint as you need to use. For a

single use, combine 1 teaspoon of cinnabar powder with ½ a teaspoon of the egg liquid, and adjust by slowly adding more liquid until the consistency is like double/heavy cream. Mix until the pigment powder is fully incorporated, and no lumps remain.

4 While these freshly made paints will not keep for long, you can store your egg mixture in the refrigerator for up to 1 week, and cinnabar pigment can be kept in an airtight container for years to come.

DRAGON'S BLOOD INK

Dragon's blood ink is one of the magical ink recipes that you may have seen in occult shops and magical recipes. This formula is referenced in ancient magical texts, medieval grimoires, and modern Wiccan charms, and refers to a simple two-ingredient ink made from the dragon's blood plant. This ink is fragranced, permanent, and possesses a rich red pigment that writes beautifully from pens, quills, and paintbrushes. There is just one problem. Over 20 different species of plants are referred to as "dragon's blood", and the resins of these plants vary widely in chemical makeup, with some having the telltale red pigment, and others lacking in colourfastness and the required solubility.

If you've ever tried to make your own dragon's blood ink at home, you may have noticed that many of the available recipes online fail to produce a useful end product. This is because many different types of dragon's blood are available on the market, typically from either the *Daemonorops draco* plant, or the *Dracaena cinnabari/Dracaena draco* plant. While both resins are technically dragon's blood, only resin from the *Dracaena* genus will be alcohol-soluble, with D. cinnabari being the ink-producing species most likely referenced in ancient and medieval texts. For this recipe, you will need to carefully select your dragon's blood resin, ensuring a good-quality product from the *Dracaena* variety, to ensure your final ink is pure and effective.

Tincture-based resin inks like this can be carried beautifully by a brush, but dry to a sticky, tacky consistency. Where soap and water fails to remove it, alcohol will dissolve the viscous resins in a pinch, so keep a small jar of alcohol on hand for cleaning brushes and workstations when using this ink.

Makes: about 3 tablespoons of ink
Prep time: 10 minutes, plus 1 week infusing

FOR THE INK
* 10g/0.25oz dragon's blood resin
* Pestle and mortar
* 30g/1oz high-proof grain alcohol
* Airtight jar
* Coffee filter
* Small airtight vessel

1 Finely powder the dragon's blood resin using a pestle and mortar, and add it to a clean airtight jar. Pour the alcohol over the powder and stir the mixture until the resin begins to dissolve.

2 Seal the jar and give it a shake, before allowing the mixture to infuse for 1 week, or until all the resin has been dissolved by the alcohol. Shake the jar daily to incorporate any resin that has not yet dissolved.

3 If after one week, there is some material that has not fully dissolved, this may indicate impurities in your dragon's blood resin. These can be strained from the liquid using a coffee filter. To test the pigment, dip a small strip of paper into the liquid and allow it to dry. If it is too weak for your project, add more powdered dragon's blood resin to the liquid and repeat the process again.

4 When you are satisfied with the colour of your ink, strain the liquid through a coffee filter to remove any sediment, and store the ink in a small airtight vessel. This ink is alcohol-based, so no additional preservatives are necessary, but you should always close the jar completely, as alcohol can evaporate, leaving your ink dry. If this happens, you can add more alcohol to the jar to rehydrate the pigment.

FRUIT, VEGETABLE & BERRY INKS

Ah, the beauty of fruits within the plant kingdom! Glistening like precious jewels, tempting and succulent, sweet and delicious, and appearing in every shade of the rainbow. Because of the ever-present availability of fruits within the human diet, we can often forget that these parts of the plant perform an important biological function in botanical reproduction. Fruits are the seed-dispersal method of many plants, which rely on an interspecies collaboration in order to reproduce. In short, mobile animals must consume the fruits and deposit their seeds far away from the immobile plant, allowing new individuals to sprout at new locations, spreading the plant far and wide. This is the reason that fruits are so colourful and delicious – they must be tempting and attractive to their animal co-conspirators, so that the necessary exchange is mutually beneficial. The pigments and fragrances that we love in fruits and veg are indeed designed to call

us forth and draw us to them, and these seductive compounds can be extracted and refined in the ink-making process, allowing us to harness those same chemical magics for our own designs.

Using fresh fruits will often result in brighter, more vivid colours, as dried fruits are often exposed to heat during the drying process, which dulls the natural pigments. For example, fresh elderberries produce a rich, dark purple pigment, while dried elderberries yield a muddy, blackened brown with subtle purple undertones. For ink making, you will want to choose fruits with good natural colour, or try using the pigment-rich parts of fruits like the peels and pits. In general, these fruit-based inks are perfect for deep reds, purples, pinks, and yellows, and produce very bold pigments when used at the height of their season. Take these notes into consideration when choosing and gathering your ink plants.

Makes: 240ml/1 cup ink

Prep time: 1 hour

FOR THE INK
* 190g/1 cup plant material
* 500ml/17fl oz/2 cups water
* Small saucepan
* Coffee filter
* Mixing bowl
* Powdered gum Arabic
* 1 tablespoon vinegar or high-proof alcohol
* Airtight ink jar
* 1 clove, wintergreen extract, or essential oils

1 Place the gathered plant material and water in your saucepan, and bring to a gentle simmer over a medium-to-low flame. Simmer until the liquid is reduced by half, about 30 minutes.

2 Remove the pan from the heat and test your ink on a small strip of paper, adding more plant material and repeating the infusion if necessary to achieve a bolder colour. When you are satisfied with the colour, strain the liquid through a coffee filter into a mixing bowl, discarding the plant material.

3 While the ink is still hot, stir in powdered gum Arabic, ¼ of a teaspoon at a time, until the ink is thickened to your preference.

4 Stir in the vinegar or alcohol as a preservative.

5 Pour a small amount of this liquid into your ink jar, reserving the rest in a larger container. Place 1 whole clove or a few drops of wintergreen extract into your ink vessel to preserve this liquid further.

6 Seal the jar, give it a shake, and your botanical ink is ready for use! Be sure to label your ink with the plant names and the date of brewing. This ink can be used immediately or stored out of direct sunlight for months and years to come.

HERB & FLOWER INKS

The natural artist's palette of colour provided by herbs and flowers is unmatched within the plant kingdom. When we think of the colours found in nature, most of us are drawn to flowers first, and many of our names for colours derive from references to the natural world (like orange, rose, periwinkle, etc.). Much like the fruit inks discussed earlier (see page 103), the pigments of flowers also perform a biological function, generated by plants to call forth animal collaborators – here, pollinators. It's remarkable how much the plant kingdom relies upon the animal kingdom and vice versa, and these natural pigments are key tools used in those instinctual interactions. In a certain sense, flower pigments can be considered a form of communication between the plant and the outside world, saying in a subtle, tongueless, and ancient language, "I'm ready to meet you! Come find me, I'm here!"

Fresh herbs and flowers will often produce a brighter hue, but because they contain water, you will sometimes need to use up to twice the amount of plant material to achieve the same depth of colour. For this reason, dried herbs may work more quickly to create a richer dye, but will make richer colours harder to achieve. Many traditional dye flowers, like coreopsis, hibiscus, dahlia, and marigold, are known for their colourfastness, and produce very bold colours that are often hard to find elsewhere in nature, like blue and green shades. Since these parts of plants are more tender and delicate, they are very susceptible to overheating, so working with the lowest heat possible will allow you to achieve the brightest colours.

Makes: 240ml/1 cup ink
Prep time: 1 hour

FOR THE INK
* 60g/about 1 cup plant material
* 500ml/17fl oz/2 cups water
* Small saucepan
* Coffee filter
* Mixing bowl
* Powdered gum Arabic
* 1 tablespoon vinegar or high-proof alcohol
* Airtight ink jar
* 1 clove, wintergreen extract, or essential oils

1 Remove any extraneous plant material (stems, flower sepals, and any material that will not be used for pigment) and discard.

2 Place the plant material and water in your saucepan and bring to a gentle simmer over a low heat. Simmer until the liquid is reduced by half, about 30 minutes.

3 Remove from the heat and test your ink on a small strip of paper, adding more plant material and repeating the infusion if necessary. When you are satisfied with the colour, strain the liquid through a coffee filter into a mixing bowl and discard the plant material.

4 While the ink is still hot, stir in powdered gum Arabic, ¼ of a teaspoon at a time, until the ink is thickened to your preference.

5 Stir in the vinegar or alcohol as a preservative.

6 Pour a small amount of this liquid into your ink jar, reserving the rest in a larger container. Place 1 whole clove or a few drops of wintergreen extract or essential oils into your ink vessel to preserve this liquid further.

7 Seal the jar, give it a shake, and your botanical ink is ready for use! Be sure to label your ink with the plant names and the date of brewing. This ink can be used immediately or stored out of direct sunlight for months and years to come.

NUT, BARK & ROOT INKS

When we consider the wide array of botanical pigments available in nature, nuts, barks, and roots are not very high on the list of beauties. These parts of the plant lack the bright, flashy colours found in flowers and fruits and they are also often difficult to access and labour-intensive to harvest and process – requiring lots of chopping and drying, etc. However, what they lack in variety, these woody materials make up in potency. Nuts, barks, and roots contain tannins which act as natural fixatives for pigments and lead to rich, dark colours with excellent colourfastness. While these pigments will typically fall in the range of reds, yellows, blacks, and browns, they will be among the deepest and longest-lasting pigments that one can make at home.

Oak galls are among the most common wood inks, mixed with iron liquor, a substance made by soaking rusty metal in water, to shift the brown infusion of oak galls into a deep, permanent black. Walnut hulls, blackthorn bark, and dye-rich roots like bloodroot and madder are also excellent choices for ink making. While not technically a nut, bark, or root, inkcap mushrooms also fall into this category because they are dense and woody once dried, and have been used in ink making for millennia.

Makes: 240ml/1 cup ink
Prep time: 1 hour

FOR THE INK
* 90g/about 1 cup wood chips, bark shavings, or chopped roots
* 500ml/17fl oz/2 cups water
* Small saucepan
* Coffee filter
* Powdered gum Arabic
* 1 tablespoon vinegar or high-proof alcohol
* Airtight ink jar
* 1 clove, wintergreen extract, or essential oils

1 As this type of plant material is especially woody and fibrous, it's important to break it down significantly to achieve a proper extraction. Use a food processor, woodworking file, or scissors to help chop the plants into lentil-sized pieces.

2 Place the plant material and water in your saucepan, then bring to a gentle simmer over a medium-to-low flame. Simmer until the liquid is reduced by half, about 30 minutes.

3 Remove from the heat and strain the liquid through a coffee filter into a mixing bowl, discarding the plant material.

4 While the ink is still hot, stir in powdered gum Arabic, ¼ of a teaspoon at a time, until the ink is thickened to your preference.

5 Stir in the vinegar or alcohol as a preservative.

6 Once cooled, pour a small amount of this liquid into your ink jar. Place 1 whole clove or a few drops of wintergreen extract or essential oils into your ink vessel to preserve this liquid further.

7 Seal the jar, give it a shake, and your botanical ink is ready for use! Be sure to label your ink with the plant names and the date of brewing. This ink can be used immediately or stored out of direct sunlight for months and years to come.

TEA INKS

Among the many herbs and leaves discussed in this book, teas are prized for their unique chemical arrangements. These plants are loaded with flavour and fragrance compounds, which is why they are so delicious to consume. Tannins are probably the most prominent and easy to recognize of these compounds, giving teas their bitter flavours and leaving an astringent, mouth-drying sensation after sipping, like drinking a very dry red wine or eating underripe fruits. These tannins are also responsible for the powerful colours of tea leaves, and they also have natural fixative properties that allow these colours to stain our teacups with repeated use.

In general, black and rooibos teas produce richer, darker inks than green and white teas. While they have a more limited pigment palate than other botanicals, it is the colourfastness of the tannins that makes tea inks so unique. Tea inks will create strokes and lines that will be slow to fade, and will dry from paler shades to rich hues upon the page. Greens, reds, browns, blacks, and golds can be drawn forth from these powerful plants, creating natural pigments that are easy to make at home using accessible ingredients and commonly found equipment. In the winter, when foraging fresh botanicals is challenging or impossible, tea inks provide a useful palette of colour to play with.

Makes: 240ml/1 cup ink
Prep time: 1 hour

FOR THE INK
* 65g/about 1 cup dried tea leaves
* Pestle and mortar (optional)
* 500ml/17fl oz/2 cups water
* Small saucepan
* Coffee filter
* Powdered gum Arabic
* 1 tablespoon vinegar or high-proof alcohol
* Airtight ink jar
* 1 clove, wintergreen extract, or essential oils

1 If your tea leaves are dense or tightly compacted, as is the case with green pearl teas, consider breaking them apart with a pestle and mortar.

2 Place the tea and water in your saucepan and bring to a gentle simmer over a low flame. Too high a flame may adversely alter the colour of your ink, turning green hues brown and muddy. Simmer until the liquid is reduced by half, about 30 minutes.

3 Remove from the heat and strain the liquid through a coffee filter into a mixing vessel, discarding the tea leaves.

4 While the ink is still hot, stir in powdered gum Arabic, ¼ of a teaspoon at a time, until the ink is thickened to your preference.

5 Stir in the vinegar or alcohol as a preservative.

6 Pour a small amount of this liquid into your ink jar. Place 1 whole clove or a few drops of wintergreen extract or essential oils into your ink vessel to preserve this liquid further.

7 Seal the jar, give it a shake, and your tea ink is ready for use! Be sure to label your ink with the plant names and the date of brewing. This ink can be used immediately or stored out of direct sunlight for months and years to come.

ROSE & MYRRH INK

As you work your way through the recipes within this chapter, you will notice that the process of making ink puts you in touch with the deeper chemical workings of our plants. By extracting their pigment, we will also be liberating other properties from the botanicals, which will affect the viscosity, colourfastness, and fragrance of our finished product. Calling upon two magical aromatics revered for their fragrance within ancient spellcraft, this recipe creates a magical ink that is equally a pigment and a perfume. Rose, a plant that needs no introduction, lends a deep-red/burgundy hue and floral scent to this blend, captured within a tincture of resinous and earthy myrrh. As a natural fixative used in perfume-making for thousands of years, myrrh helps to bind the delicate fragrance of the flowers, creating a drawing ink with perfume that is harmonious and long-lasting.

As myrrh is the incense resin of chthonic spirits, it is best to start this tincture on the new moon, or on a Saturday closest to the new moon.

Makes: about 200ml/0.75 cup ink

Prep time: 10 minutes, plus 2–4 weeks infusing and 1 week further infusing

FOR THE INK

* Small airtight jars
* 115g/about ¼ cup powdered myrrh resin
* 120ml/4fl oz/½ cup high-proof grain alcohol
* Sieve/fine-mesh strainer or coffee filter
* 3 fresh whole red roses
* Scissors
* Wooden spoon/muddler

1 In a small airtight jar, stir together the powdered myrrh and alcohol. Allow to infuse for 2–4 weeks, then strain through a sieve or coffee filter and store in a clean airtight jar until ready to use.

2 On the day you wish to make your ink, gather your fresh roses and remove the petals from the sepals. Use scissors to chop these petals into smaller pieces and break open the plant's cell structure, releasing its perfume and pigment.

3 In a separate airtight jar, place your rose petals and pour 1 tablespoon of the myrrh tincture over the top. Use the back of a wooden spoon or muddler to gently pound the rose petals into the tincture, macerating them and breaking them down even further. Add more tincture bit by bit until the roses are submerged and as macerated as possible. Seal the jar and allow to infuse at least overnight, but ideally for up to 1 week.

4 Test your ink on a small strip of paper using a paint brush. The ink will be quite pale at first, but as it dries upon the page, a deeper colour will emerge. If you want a stronger pigment infusion, strain this liquid and repeat the process with three fresh roses.

5 Seal the finished ink in the airtight jar, as alcohol will evaporate over time. This ink can be used immediately or stored out of direct sunlight for months and years to come.

BOTANICAL DRAWING CHARCOALS

This chapter has extensively explored the use of various plants for artistic applications, as paints and inks in every colour and shade. We have considered fruits, flowers, leaves, and roots, minerals and botanicals, and materia from all seasons in our exploration of plant pigments. In these works, stems and twigs are often the discards of our process, typically lacking significant colour of their own, and being too dense and fibrous to create efficient extractions. However, in our hunt for recipes that explore purpose and magic in all parts of plants, these woody leftovers are not without their uses. Through careful transmutation by fire, any witch with the right equipment can roast their own drawing charcoals from nearly any woody stems, creating simple writing and artistic media from our plant allies, as part of a holistic approach to green magic that leaves no botanical materia behind.

Make sure to harvest dense, fibrous plant material like branches or vines from plants that are relevant to your practice. Grape vine, blackberry cane, oak or birch branches, or rose wood are some good choices to consider. Your harvested twigs should be at least as thick as a Sharpie marker, as thinner material could scorch and reduce to ash. You may wish to consider using specific woods for specific spells (oak for Jupiter magic, rose for love spells, blackberry for protection magic, etc.), but be sure to carefully package and label your charcoals, as your stems will be quite fragile and very similar in appearance after roasting.

Makes: about 10–20 charcoals
Prep time: 2 hours

FOR THE INK

* Short lengths of dense, woody twigs or vines
* Clean, empty paint can with lid (or closed metal container of similar size)
* Hammer and large, thick nail
* Firewood or charcoal
* Fire pit or grill

I Cut your harvested branches to a length that will fit securely in your paint can, and add as many as you can while still allowing air flow within the vessel. This metal can will act as an oven or kiln, roasting the twigs to a perfect black charcoal, without direct use of flames.

2 To help air circulate within the paint can, use a hammer and a thick nail to poke holes in the base and lid of the can – five holes in each (four around the edges and one in the centre) should be enough.

3 Place the paint can in the centre of a fire pit or grill, and heap wood or charcoal around the can. Be sure to cover the top and sides completely. Light the fire and allow to burn for 30 minutes to 1 hour. You may remove the can from the fire to check your charcoals after 30 minutes, but it is important to allow the can to cool before opening. If the charcoals are not finished, reseal the can and return it to the fire for additional 30-minute increments.

4 Once cooled, these charcoals can be trimmed to fine points and used immediately, dry or with water.

Paper

Paper

aper is an unlikely candidate for the greatest human invention. It is fragile, humble, and expendable in the modern world, where we encounter perfectly smooth, affordable paper on a daily basis. In fact, paper is so cheap and ubiquitous that it makes up a good bulk of the disposable packaging in our world. For most of human history, this was not so, and the laborious process of crafting paper from plant fibres made this substance quite rare and valuable. Paper as we know it today was a late arrival in the West; it was developed in China in the 1st and 2nd centuries CE, but was not adopted in Europe until as late as the 11th century. This invention made it possible to record history and disseminate knowledge with far greater ease, enabling the process of industrial printing and making paper goods accessible to the common people. In this sense, paper is how we know our history, how we learn from the past, and how we communicate with those who came before, by interacting with the books and documents made possible only by the production of paper. From Ancient Egyptian papyrus to early hand-bound medieval manuscripts, it is to paper and the fibre-rich plants that make it possible that we as humans owe so very much.

But more than just allowing us to preserve our writing cheaply and efficiently, paper holds deeper meaning for animist witches. In this context, paper represents a collaborative relationship between plants and their human kin. Before plant-based paper in Europe, the most common writing surface was animal skin parchment, or traditional vellum. This requires not just the slaughter of a valuable animal, but a lengthy process of stretching, moulding, and drying the skin. In contrast, plant papers require us to use only the macerated fibres, which are a much more renewable, and bloodless, resource. These plant allies have been trusted as the keepers of our history, our stories, and all the mundane notes of our lives, everything from shopping lists to the Holy Bible. They have enabled us as human practitioners to engage in a form of time travel made possible only by books, paper, and the way they allow us to share information across decades and centuries. By cultivating a relationship with these plants, we cultivate a relationship with the future.

However, while the papermaking process no longer requires the blood sacrifice of animal life, it is not without its own costs. The amount of plant material called for in this book should raise some important questions in your mind, especially about the nature of allyship within the context of an honourable harvest. How can we both honour a plant and kill it? If these plants are our sacred spirit allies, how can we justify their harvest? This is one of the truths of being alive as a human, that in order to live, we must consume other beings. While traditions of honourable harvest and respectful culling can teach us much about the energetic exchange between plants and people, some crafts will always appear to be a net negative for our natural kin. Papermaking, which relies on killing trees and other plants, is one such practice. For this reason, it's very important to be mindful of how much we take, and to offset our harvest with offerings to spirits, the replanting of harvested plants, and regenerative foraging practices, like those outlined in the introduction to this book.

In ancient magic, specific papers were more heavily emphasized in spellwork, with hieratic, or priestly, papyrus being overwhelmingly preferred in most Mediterranean charms. This paper was first developed in Egypt from the Cyperus papyrus plant, a marsh-dwelling relative of rushes and sedges. It is cited for making talismans and amulets within the *Greek Magical Papyri*, where a spell may have included drawing and consecrating an image on papyrus as the principal route to manifestation, with no other materials required for the charm. There are many such operations which rely on figurative spells, drawn on paper and carried as amulets. In the medieval grimoires, word squares like the SATOR Square and those found within the *Book of Abramelin* often work this way (see page 114).

Islamic magic is rich in figurative charms, laid out in the traditions of the Koranic amulets and talisman-making books like the *Picatrix*. The stave symbols of Icelandic magic are also specifically noted as having been drawn on paper, so that they could be easily and discreetly carried and employed. In hoodoo and rootwork, the names and images drawn on petition papers are used to create energetic links with distant targets, or actualize outcomes by working with these paper talismans. Many magical alphabets, like Theban or the Runic scripts, require their letters to be written to be effective for magical purposes. We can think of modern sigil magic much the same way, in which the drawing of the witch's sigil is the primary modality for actualizing one's will. In all these cases, the required ritual materials are only papers and ink, speaking to the incredible power and popularity of using paper as a magical tool, as a blank substance for absorbing and containing the will of the magician.

With this context in mind, it's easy to see the emphasis placed on magical books throughout history. If writing a word or an image can capture our will and contain the power of our desires, then a written book made of thousands of such images could contain unlimited power and potential. For magic books, containing countless talismanic symbols and magical marks, these pages are the bearers of a well of sorcerous potency that can be tapped into and approached by the reader simply by turning the pages. By printing our will in text and images, we not only give these intentions permanence, we also bind ourselves to them inextricably. These grimoires and books of spells have been variously praised and demonized throughout history, specifically because they carry within their pages illicit wisdom and ritual marks. These act as portals to transformative knowledge and gnosis with the divine, such that it was believed some books were haunted by spirits and devils, being bound to those who read their words. Some authors even used textual spells inscribed in their books to keep them safe and preserve the knowledge within, such as the history of medieval book curses, written in margins and covers by monks and scribes, as a preventative measure against library theft.

But what many of these sources for textual chams and paper magic often leave out is a direct mention of the plants involved in their creation. We can sometimes find traditions that emphasize specific plants for magical papermaking, such as the Otomí bark paper called "amate" used in indigenous Mexican brujeria, but this level of specificity is hard to find in Western magic. More often, Western occultism shows us paper as a blank and holy vessel for receiving, whether that be used to preserve our writing, draw talismans, write charms, or bind inspirited books of magic.

Word Squares

As an example of textual magic, take a look at these word squares from *The Book of Abramelin*.[ix] These are written on paper and used as talismans to achieve various ends. The first is used to discover another witch's magic, the second to learn all things of the past and future, and the third to see visions in the moon.

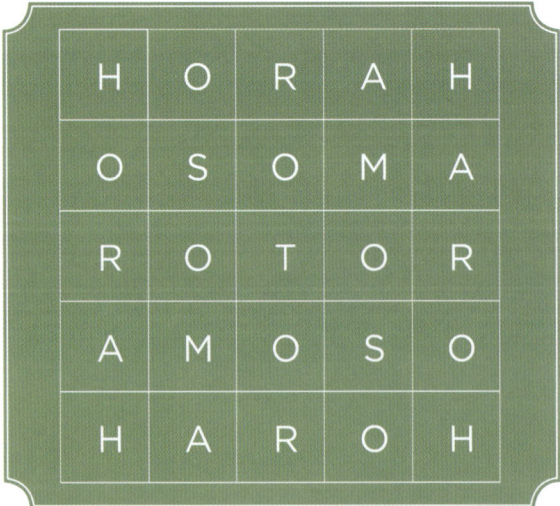

In the recipes ahead, you will find a departure from this tradition, looking at papers which are defined by the plants that make them, and are used as portals for engaging with those allies. There are recipes that create papers for the various seasons, making printable seed paper for charms that grow our magic in a literal sense, and even techniques for binding your own magical journals and mini grimoires. Since this book is designed to deepen our relationship with plants through working with them as magical tools, I encourage you to explore papermaking from this animist perspective and to carry a deep respect and gratitude for these fabulous fibre plants into all your harvesting.

Paper tools

Before beginning the recipes ahead, it's important to make sure you have all the ingredients and equipment on hand. While many of the crafts in this book can be worked with objects you already have at home, papermaking is a specialized arte and necessitates some specialized tools. For this craft, you will need:

* **MOULD AND DECKLE** – This is the most important and highly specialized piece of papermaking equipment. A mould and deckle allows us to form our paper pulp into fine, even sheets. The deckle is a wooden frame holding a sheet of fine mesh, meant to separate our plant fibres from the water of our paper slurry. The mould is a simple wooden frame of the same size, which sits atop the deckle to form the shape of our paper sheets. These tools are very affordable and easy to find, but you can easily make your own mould and deckle out of wood and any sturdy scrap mesh you have, like window screening or fine

hardware cloth. This can be especially handy for creating custom paper shapes and sizes that are fully unique to your craft.

* **SLURRY BIN** – No matter what size of paper you're creating, you will need to create a slurry, or a mix of paper pulp and water. This slurry bin is where our mould and deckle pulls our paper sheets from, and it needs to be large enough to submerge the mould and deckle completely. Large bowls, plastic tubs, or any other large, waterproof container will do.

* **BLENDER** – Our paper pulp needs to be lump-free in order to create even sheets of paper. In order to achieve a smooth, even consistency in our paper pulp, using a blender, immersion blender, or food processor is essential.

- **CANVAS OR FABRIC SHEETS** – When we dry paper sheets, we want to do so on a surface that will maintain the smooth, even surface created by our deckle. Drying our paper using a smooth, tight-weave fabric like canvas will make sure our finished papers are flat and ready for use.

- **SPONGE OR TOWEL** – Essential for removing excess moisture and speeding the drying process.

How to make paper

In order to talk about the details of paper crafting, we need to talk about plant fibres first. These tissues are produced by plants as support structures, allowing a plant to stand tall and rigid, and to withstand the gusts of wind and trampling of animals as it grows throughout the year. Fibres can be found in all parts of plants, from leaves to stalks to roots to fruits, but not all plants will possess them in the same concentration. For example, coconut and palm fruits are incredibly fibre-rich, while tomato plants produce fibre-rich stems instead, to withstand the weight of ripened fruit. Plant fibres are fully developed when a plant reaches maturity, and do not rot in the same way that other plant structures do. After a plant dies and many of its tissues are washed away, the fibres often remain behind, taking much longer to break down. This means fibres have fabulous longevity when dried and cared for properly, making textiles, twine, and fabrics which will last for years and years.

When making paper, these are the parts of plants we want to isolate. To do this, many paper-making recipes involve cooking or fermenting our plants, to break down and wash away all plant tissues that are not fibrous in nature. In the final stages of the paper-making process, these fibres are allowed to layer over one another, creating a fibre matrix, which dries to produce thin sheets of paper. This matrix, with fibres crossing in every direction, is what makes paper so durable, allowing it to hold its shape and withstand writing and erasing. Without these interlocking fibres, paper would be brittle and fragile.

The recipes ahead will steer you in the direction of plants that are fibre-rich enough for this process, but there are

simple ways to identify if a plant will be suitable for papermaking. Grasses and trees are plants which are known for producing lots of fibre, particularly in grass stems and tree barks. Other plants produce fibres in their stems and leaves, and can be identified by gently ripping or cutting the plant cross-wise. Leaves with lots of fibre, like yucca, irises, or daffodils, will be difficult to tear, while fibrous stalks like nettle, mugwort, honeysuckle, or hemp will be almost impossible to cut without scissors. This is a testament to how strong plant fibres can be! Woodier, thicker stems will require more fermentation or breaking down in order to be usable for paper, so fibrous leaves and grasses may be more suitable for beginners to use. It's a fun experiment to explore your local bioregion and take note of fibre-rich plants in your area, revealing the paper-making powerhouses living right within your landscape.

With your plants harvested, you're ready to begin the paper-making process. This procedure is a general overview of the process, while individual recipes within this chapter will outline specific recommended steps, as there is some room for variation. For best results, follow these recipe steps carefully, but feel free to use this metric as a baseline for conducting your own paper-making experiments.

STEP 1 – Prepare your fibres

Plant-based paper can be made from both dry or fresh botanicals, but in both cases, our fibres require preparation. Fresh plants will often need to be cooked or fermented, so that soluble plant parts, which would otherwise make our paper fragile and thick, are discarded. Adding gentle natural caustics like soda ash to our stock pots or fermentation vessels may be preferable here, as it can help speed up the breakdown of woodier stalks and vines, but gloves and good ventilation are required to work with these compounds. For most tender plants, simmering them in warm water until fork-tender (soft enough to pull apart but not sloppy and disintegrating) will be enough to break them down. Rinse this plant material until all soft and slimy discards are washed away, leaving only the fibrous plant material behind.

STEP 2 –
Create paper pulp

With fibres washed and ready, it's time to break them down into sizes suitable for paper-making. In order to produce the fibre matrix which makes good paper, we will need to cut these fibres into small pieces and create a uniform slurry, called pulp. To create your paper pulp, use scissors to cut your fibrous plants into small pieces and place them in a blender. For beginner papermakers, I find that adding a bit of pre-soaked scrap paper (newspaper, printer paper, construction paper – any paper you like) will help create a better final texture. Think of this scrap paper as a "seed", since it contains the smooth, even texture we're hoping to create. This will fill any gaps between your plant fibres and is a useful way to recycle paper waste you already have around the house. Aim for a 1:1 or 2:1 ratio between your plant fibres and scrap paper. Add this paper to your blender, and process with as much water as needed to create an evenly blended pulp. The evenness of your pulp texture will determine the smoothness of your paper, so be careful not to rush this step.

STEP 3 –
Create paper sheets

This next step will be our most labour-intensive, and it does require a bit of special equipment. Most importantly, a mould and deckle will be essential for forming our paper sheets. This is basically a wooden frame with a removable screen on the bottom, which allows us to capture and evenly disperse small amounts of paper pulp to create thin, even sheets. You will also need a container (tub, bowl or bin, for example) deep and wide enough to submerge your mould and deckle. I find that plastic storage bins work well for this, and they are easy to clean and repurpose after use.

Transfer all the paper pulp to your slurry bin and fill with enough water to create a depth that can submerge your mould and deckle – about 1.5–2.5cm/4–6in. Holding your mould and deckle together firmly, gently dip one end into the slurry, trapping a bit of the mixture in the frame of the mould. Use the water to mix this slurry back and forth, tilting and moving your deckle left to right, up and down, until the pulp is evenly spread across the deckle's screen. If you do not have enough pulp within the deckle to do this, add more slurry. This will dry to become your paper sheet, so make sure no holes or lumps are present. It may take some practice to determine the precise thickness needed.

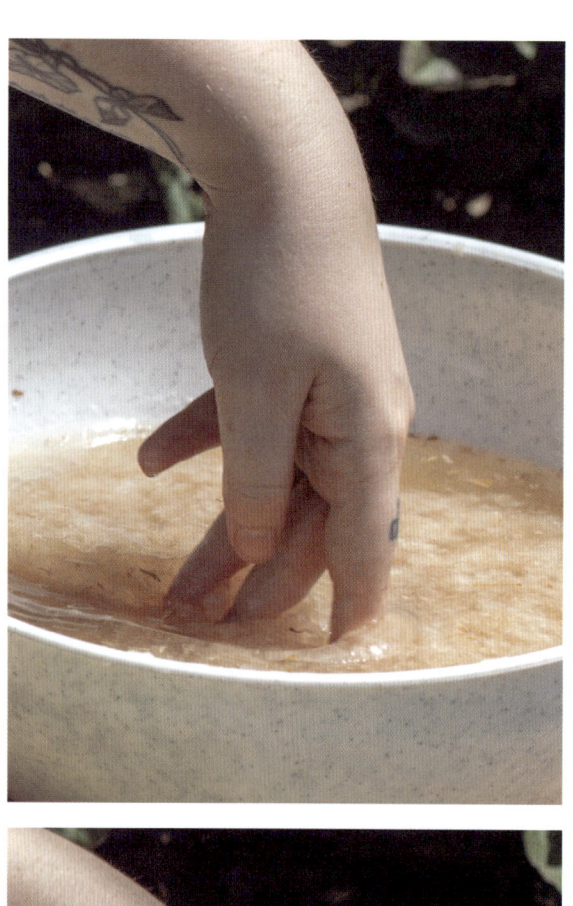

STEP 4 –
Dry your paper

When you are satisfied with the layer of pulp, lift the mould and deckle out of the water, and set the mould frame aside. To dry your paper, a sheet of canvas or finely woven fabric (like a sheet or pillowcase) is necessary. This will allow the water to evaporate from the paper, but will keep the plant fibres from moving after they are moulded. This fabric should always be damp when used for papermaking, so that it dries at the same rate as our paper. Lay out your damp sheet of canvas or fabric on a flat surface, ensuring that it has no wrinkles.

Lay the deckle face-down onto the fabric. Use a sponge or towel to dab the back of the deckle screen, removing as much water as you can before carefully lifting the deckle away. You should see an evenly square sheet of plant fibres left behind. For best results, lay out as many sheets of paper on your fabric as possible, then dry these sheets until they can be safely removed. Gently peel these sheets away from the fabric, allow to dry completely, then store flat until ready to use.

As you move through the recipes in this chapter, keep these guidelines in mind. You will undoubtedly notice some variation here and there with the techniques used to unlock the fibres in the specific plants. Because each plant has a unique composition, this kind of discernment will be necessary for your own experiments with other plants. These recipes will also help expand your paper-making prowess, using natural dye plants to create coloured papers, using scrap paper to create paper clay sculptures, and teaching simple threading techniques for binding your own journals and grimoires from handmade paper. With the basics down, there is much room for experimenting and artistry, to create new and exciting paper crafts beyond the recipes this book contains.

WILDFLOWER SEED PAPER

There are very few ways to create a "green" paper or publication. As a practice, papermaking relies upon killing trees and plants for their leaves and stalks, making it very hard or impossible to offset the required environmental damage. However, there are small actions we can take that offset this necessary harvest, returning the energetic exchange to the living earth itself. One way we can do this is by creating seed paper from otherwise discarded paper scraps, which can then be planted to grow new life. While this will not replace the plants we've harvested, it will allow us to recycle our paper waste and plant regenerative plants in their place, returning their carbon to the natural cycle of growth and decay, and introducing beneficial new plants that will feed the ecosystem as a whole.

As a quick note about seed paper, this is best produced with seeds that are as small as possible, so that the finished paper is not lumpy. Chamomile, cornflower, poppy, alyssum, yarrow, mint, basil, coreopsis, and other plants with very small seeds would be great choices for this project. If you are using a store-bought wildflower seed blend and you notice some seeds are too large, use a colander or sieve to sift them out.

Prep time: 30 minutes, plus drying

FOR THE PAPER

* 30g/about 2 cups shredded paper
* 500ml/17fl oz/2 cups hot water
* Blender
* Slurry bin
* Mould and deckle
* Wildflower seed blend
* Damp sheet of canvas or fabric
* Sponge or towel

1 Add the shredded paper and hot water to a blender, and process on high speed until evenly mixed to a pulp. There should be no large pieces remaining.

2 Transfer this pulp to your slurry bin and add enough water to submerge your mould and deckle. Stir in your wildflower seeds. Dip your mould and deckle into the slurry, then slowly raise them out of the liquid, tilting the deckle to evenly disperse the paper fibres.

3 When you are satisfied with the thickness of your sheet, gently transfer the deckle face-down to your flat, damp sheet of canvas or fabric. Use a sponge or towel to dab liquid away from the back of the deckle, and gently lift it away.

4 Repeat until you have used as much of the slurry as possible.

5 Allow these new sheets of paper to solidify before carefully peeling away from the canvas. Hang the paper sheets up to dry completely, then store flat in a dry place until ready to use.

NATURAL COLOURED PAPER

Coloured paper can be a fabulous addition to any project. As a cover for hand-bound journals, decorative paper for greeting cards, or even just as a fabulous DIY exercise, making coloured paper adds a unique challenge to standard papermaking techniques. Since this book is focused on botanical craft, we'll be steering clear of synthetic dyes and colourants for this project, opting instead for the pigments of natural plants, which will lend their hue to our paper fibres. The addition of soy milk helps these colours to bind to the fibres quickly and easily, without using stronger chemical mordants (see pages 61–7 for further discussion of mordants and dye plants). Before you begin, select the dye plants you want to work with and ensure that these are dried and powdered as finely as possible.

Beyond using these colourful papers in craft work, they are also valuable as materia magica. The same way coloured candles, inks, and clothing are used as anchors for the psyche in ritual magic, coloured papers can be used for writing petitions, drawing seals, or inscribing textual or image charms. These papers contain an added dose of plant magic, calling in our dye plants as allies toward whatever magical needs arise.

Prep time: 2 hours 30 minutes, plus drying

FOR THE PAPER

* 30g/about 2 cups shredded paper
* 60ml/¼ cup soy milk
* Blender
* 5 tablespoons powdered dye plants
* 500ml/17fl oz/2 cups hot water
* Mould and deckle
* Slurry bin
* Damp sheet of canvas or fabric
* Sponge or towel

I Soak the shredded paper in the soy milk and enough water to fully submerge the paper for 30 minutes. Strain and gently squeeze excess liquid from your paper fibres before transferring to your blender.

2 Next, prepare your paper dye. Mix the dye power and hot water together and allow to infuse for 30 minutes. If you want to test the strength of the dye, dip a test strip into the dye bath for a few seconds before allowing to dry. You can add more powdered dye plants if you like, increasing the depth of colour.

3 When you are satisfied with the strength of your pigment, pour the hot dye over the paper pulp in your blender and stir to combine. Allow to stand, covered, until the dye liquid cools completely, about 1 hour.

4 Process your dyed paper fibres on high speed until evenly mixed to a pulp.

5 Transfer this pulp to your slurry bin and add enough water to submerge your mould and deckle. Dip your mould and deckle into the slurry, then slowly raise them out of the liquid, tilting the deckle to evenly disperse the paper fibres.

6 When you are satisfied with the thickness of your sheet, gently transfer the deckle face-down to your flat, damp sheet of canvas or fabric. Use a sponge or towel to dab liquid away from the back of the deckle, and gently lift it away.

7 Repeat until you have used as much of the slurry as possible.

8 Allow these new sheets of paper to solidify before carefully peeling away from the canvas. Hang the paper sheets up to dry completely, then store flat in a dry place until ready to use.

JAPANESE KNOTWEED PAPER

Once an obscure wayside plant, Japanese knotweed is now a household name in most parts of the world. This plant has earned its fame as one of the most tenaciously invasive plants of the 21st century, being nearly impossible to eradicate and quite disruptive to environments outside of Asia. When introduced to a new landscape with no natural predators, knotweed thrives as an intruder, and drives native plants from the environment. On residential property, knotweed shoots can be so strong that they can damage the foundation of a home if planted too closely. While much of this environmental damage is more than one individual can combat, we can do our best to curtail knotweed's efforts by liberally harvesting the plant for food, crafts, and magical operations.

Even as an invasive, this plant is still quite valuable, packed with nutrients, vitamins, and, for our purposes, beautiful fibres for papermaking. Harvesting the stalks will be a solid effort in beating back this weed, especially if undertaken before the plant begins to flower in late summer. While this harvest won't kill the knotweed plants, it can help stop them from reproducing, slowing their spread through fragile native ecosystems. In a rare case of win-win, harvesting this plant benefits both the environment and our crafting process. The stems will have the most fibre, producing stronger paper. Because this recipe requires a gentle caustic soda ash powder, it is best to work in a well-ventilated area with proper PPE.

Prep time: 2 hours, plus drying

FOR THE PAPER

* 1lb Japanese knotweed stems, cut to 1cm/½in pieces
* Stock pot
* Water
* 1 teaspoon soda ash
* Colander
* Blender
* 15g/about 1 cup shredded paper, pre-soaked
* Mould and deckle
* Slurry bin
* Damp sheet of canvas or fabric
* Sponge or towel

1 Add your knotweed stems to a stock pot and cover with water.

2 Stir the soda ash into the stock pot, then bring to a gentle simmer. Cook until the plants are fork-tender, when the fibres just begin to pull apart easily.

3 When cooked and softened, transfer your knotweed to a colander and rinse thoroughly until the water runs clear.

4 In a blender, combine your cooked knotweed fibres with the pre-soaked shredded paper. Add enough water to just cover the plants and paper, and process on high speed until evenly mixed to a pulp. There should be no large pieces of knotweed remaining.

5 Transfer this pulp to your slurry bin and add enough water to submerge your mould and deckle. Dip your mould and deckle into the slurry and slowly raise them out of the liquid, tilting the deckle to evenly disperse the paper fibres.

6 When you are satisfied with the thickness of your sheet, gently transfer the deckle face-down to your flat, damp canvas or pillowcase. Use a sponge or towel to dab liquid away from the back of the deckle, and gently lift it away.

7 Repeat until you have used as much of the knotweed slurry as possible.

8 Allow these new sheets of paper to solidify before carefully peeling away from the canvas. Hang the paper sheets up to dry completely, then store flat in a dry place until ready to use.

WHOLE-HERB MUGWORT PAPER

Mugwort is a name every witch should know. This plant is one of the classic "witching herbs" of Europe, associated with witchcraft and magic right down to its Latin nomenclature, *Artemisia*, after the Ancient Greek moon goddess Artemis. This plant induces vivid dreams, aids in divinations, and is used medicinally in the regulation of the menstrual cycle, all adding to its lunar correspondence. Luckily for us, this plant is also very invasive throughout most of the temperate world, making it a safe choice for harvesting in large quantities, without fear of negatively impacting the environment around us . In all likelihood, you can probably find some mugwort growing somewhere in your neighborhood, so this recipe will be a good occasion to acquaint yourself with the witching herbs growing just outside your front door! Like many plants, the stems of mugwort will have the most fibre, producing stronger paper, so try to select tall, stately plants with strong stems.

Since its primary ingredient is an herb of the moon, this mugwort paper is perfect for making lunar talismans or textual charms. Consider binding these pages into a journal for recording dreams and divinations, or saving mugwort paper pulp for sculpting into altar adornments (see page 136 for instructions on sculpting with paper clay).

Prep time: 2 hours, plus drying

FOR THE PAPER

* 450g/1lb mugwort plants, inclusive of stems, leaves, and roots
* Hammer
* 2 stock pots
* Water
* Colander
* 15g/about 1 cup shredded paper, pre-soaked
* Blender
* Mould and deckle
* Slurry bin
* Damp sheet of canvas or fabric
* Sponge or towel

1 Separate the leaves, roots, and stems of the mugwort, as these are processed separately. Using a hammer, pound your stems and roots on a sturdy surface until the fibres begin to open up and soften.

2 Next, prepare your fibres by gently cooking them. In a stock pot, simmer the leaves in enough water to cover them until they are soft and the small stems at the base of the leaves pull apart easily.

3 In a second stock pot, simmer your stems and roots in enough water to cover them until they are fork-tender but not mushy.

4 When cooked and softened, transfer your mugwort to a colander and rinse thoroughly until the water runs clear.

5 In a blender, combine your cooked leaves, your tender roots and stems with the pre-soaked shredded paper. Add enough water to just cover the plants and paper, and process on high speed until evenly mixed to a pulp. There should be no large pieces of mugwort remaining.

6 Transfer this pulp to your slurry bin and add enough water to submerge your mould and deckle. Dip your mould and deckle into the slurry and slowly raise them out of the liquid, tilting the deckle to evenly disperse the paper fibres.

7 When you are satisfied with the thickness of your sheet, gently transfer the deckle face-down to your flat damp canvas or pillowcase. Use a sponge or towel to dab liquid away from the back of the deckle, and gently lift it away.

8 Repeat until you have used as much of the mugwort slurry as possible.

9 Allow these new sheets of paper to solidify before carefully peeling away from the canvas. Hang the paper sheets up to dry completely, then store flat in a dry place until ready to use.

SPRING EQUINOX DANDELION PAPER

Dandelions are the heralds of spring, the emissaries of Venus as she makes her return to the landscape. When spring arrives with her psychedelic sprays of colour, the dandelion (from the French for "lion's tooth", *le dent de lion*) is among the first to appear. Bold despite their size, these tenacious, weedy plants are rich in medicinal value, and steeped in magical folklore and history. This solary herb is said to aid in divination and the delivery of prophecy, and returning lost lovers. It has even been used for a simple, natural method of telling the time and the weather; because the plant opens at dawn, and closes just before dusk or a storm, shepherds have used the dandelion to know when to call their sheep home, and when to keep them safely out of the field. The stems will have the most fibre, producing stronger paper, so try to harvest stems and flowers in a ratio of 5:1 by weight. For 900g/2lb of total bounty, this means about 700g/1lb 9oz of dandelion stems, and 200g/7oz of flowers.

Prep time: 30 minutes, plus 2–3 days drying, soaking overnight, and final drying

FOR THE PAPER

* 900g/2lb fresh foraged dandelion flowers and stems (700g/1lb 9oz stems and 200g/7oz flowers)
* Water
* Stock pot
* 30g/about 2 cups shredded paper
* Blender
* Mould and deckle
* Slurry bin
* Damp canvas or cloth
* Sponge or towel

1 Dry the dandelion flowers and stems in the sun until all water is removed, about 2–3 days.

2 Once dry, cut the stems into 1cm pieces. Soak the stems and flowers overnight in water to soften.

3 The following day, combine your soaked dandelion and the pre-soaked shredded paper in a blender. Add enough water to just cover the plants and paper, and process on high speed until evenly mixed to a pulp. There should be no large pieces of dandelion stem remaining.

4 Transfer this pulp to your slurry bin and add enough water to submerge your mould and deckle. Dip your mould and deckle into the slurry and slowly raise them out of the liquid, tilting the deckle to evenly disperse the paper fibres.

5 When you are satisfied with the thickness of your sheet, gently transfer the deckle face-down to your flat, damp canvas or pillowcase. Use a sponge or towel to dab liquid away from the back of the deckle, and gently lift it away.

6 Repeat until you have used as much of the dandelion slurry as possible.

7 Allow these new sheets of paper to solidify before carefully peeling away from the canvas. Hang the paper sheets up to dry completely, then store flat in a dry place until ready to use.

SUMMER SOLSTICE ROSE PAPER

As the year ripens, flowers emerge as the heralds of autumn's harvest, and the rose is given special reverence as the queen of the summer blossoms. Aromatic, lush, flavourful, and richly hued, the rose is generous with her gifts, and has entranced humans for millennia with her almost divine beauty. In green magic, the rose is not just emblematic of love and seduction (areas in which she reigns supreme), but also of protection magic and all manner of Venusian evocation. As an ally to the witch, the rose is called upon in glamoury, persuasion, reconciliation magic, divination, and blessing charms, as one of the most storied and useful herbs within the witch's garden. In summer, these flowers are at their most fragrant and abundant, especially toward the end of June, near the summer solstice. This summer solstice paper is an exercise in capturing the intensity and illumination of this solar holiday, using the rose as an avatar of the season – it is summer incarnate.

Rose petals are quite tender, and do not have too much of their own natural fibre, so we need to fortify them with shredded paper as well for this recipe, creating a smooth finished paper that is speckled with the natural colour of the rose.

Prep time: 30 minutes, plus 2–3 days drying, soaking overnight, and final drying

FOR THE PAPER
* 225g/8oz fresh rose petals
* Water
* Stock pot
* 30g/about 2 cups shredded paper
* Blender
* Mould and deckle
* Slurry bin
* Damp canvas or cloth
* Sponge or towel

1 Dry the rose petals in the sun until all water is removed, about 2–3 days.

2 Once dry, soak the petals overnight in water to soften.

3 The following day, combine your soaked rose and the pre-soaked shredded paper in a blender. Add enough water to just cover the plants and paper, and process on high speed until evenly mixed to a pulp. There should be no large pieces of rose remaining.

4 Transfer this pulp to your slurry bin and add enough water to submerge your mould and deckle. Dip your mould and deckle into the slurry and slowly raise them out of the liquid, tilting the deckle to evenly disperse the paper fibres.

5 When you are satisfied with the thickness of your sheet, gently transfer the deckle face-down to your flat, damp canvas or pillowcase. Use a sponge or towel to dab liquid away from the back of the deckle, and gently lift it away.

6 Repeat until you have used as much of the slurry as possible.

7 Allow these new sheets of paper to solidify before carefully peeling away from the canvas. Hang the paper sheets up to dry completely, then store flat in a dry place until ready to use.

AUTUMN EQUINOX CORN HUSK PAPER

In the northern hemisphere, autumn is the harvest season, signalling a culmination in the warmth and activity of the agricultural year. In the United States where I live, this means endless fields of tall sweetcorn, drying and yellowing in the fading sun as the grains within ripen. Corn is an indigenous crop to this continent, responsible for the survival of countless generations, and is one of the sacred "three sisters" of Iroquois and Cherokee gardens. In Europe, corn is under the rulership of Saturn, the planet of endings, limits, and the rot which yields rebirth. In German folklore, corn fields are believed to be inhabited by satyr-like "buckmen" or corn-spirits, which haunt and protect the fields.

In respect to the sanctity of this holy crop, our paper recipe uses corn husks, which are ordinarily discarded as waste. These fibre-rich leaves are perfect for papermaking, and help make use of plant materia which often goes unnoticed. As a magical exercise, this recipe demonstrates that all aspects of our plants have inherent value, as long as we are creative enough to unlock their material and magical potential. Because this recipe requires a gentle caustic soda ash powder, it is best to work in a well-ventilated area.

Prep time: 1 hour, plus drying

FOR THE PAPER

* 225g/8oz dried corn husks
* Scissors
* Stock pot
* Water
* 1 teaspoon soda ash
* Colander
* 15g/about 1 cup shredded paper, pre-soaked
* Blender
* Mould and deckle
* Slurry bin
* Damp canvas or cloth
* Sponge or towel

1 Prepare your corn husk fibres by gently cooking them. Use scissors to trim your husks into 1cm/½in pieces, then combine them in a stock pot with enough water to cover.

2 Wearing a mask and gloves, stir in the soda ash, and gently simmer until the plant fibres pull apart easily but are not mushy.

3 When fully cooked and softened, transfer your corn husks to a colander and rinse thoroughly until the water runs clear.

4 In a blender, combine your cooked corn husks and the pre-soaked shredded paper. Add enough water to just cover the plants and paper, and process on high speed until evenly mixed to a pulp. There should be no large pieces of husk remaining.

5 Transfer this pulp to your slurry bin and add enough water to submerge your mould and deckle. Dip your mould and deckle into the slurry and slowly raise them out of the liquid, tilting the deckle to evenly disperse the paper fibres.

6 When you are satisfied with the thickness of your sheet, gently transfer the deckle face-down to your flat, damp canvas or pillowcase. Use a sponge or towel to dab liquid away from the back of the deckle, and gently lift it away.

7 Repeat until you have used as much of the slurry as possible.

8 Allow these new sheets of paper to solidify before carefully peeling away from the canvas. Hang the paper sheets up to dry completely, then store flat in a dry place until ready to use.

WINTER SOLSTICE BIRCH BARK PAPER

Birch is the guardian of winter forests, and a tree of magic and protection, lighting up the landscape and offering a useful array of craft tools, foods, and medicines during the long grey winter season. However, among the myriad attributes of this unique tree, it is the iconic ethereal white bark of the birch tree that has earned it historic fame. The bark can be removed in flexible, durable sheets, which have been used to make everything from paper and baskets to canoes. This has earned white birch the moniker "paper birch", and these shaggy layers of bark can be seen peeling on their own throughout most of the year, offering themselves up in a way that suggests their many uses to human eyes.

Unlike our other papermaking methods presented in this chapter, our birch paper will be almost entirely natural, with no additives or lengthy processing required. We find books make from this kind of paper everywhere that birch grows, but especially in the Middle East, Eastern Europe, and North America. The oldest surviving manuscripts date to the 1st century CE, attesting to the remarkable natural preservatives found within birch bark. Gather this bark from fallen or dead trees, or in the last weeks of winter when the sap begins to run and the bark is soft and flexible. If harvesting large amounts of birch, try to harvest small quantities from multiple trees, as each tree will need to heal from the harvest.

Prep time: 1 hour, plus soaking overnight and drying

FOR THE PAPER
* Large sheets of birch bark, harvested sustainably
* Soap
* Sponge
* Stock pot
* Paper towels
* Drying weights or heavy books

1 To harvest the birch bark, select areas that are flat and even, with few cracks, knots, or bits of lichen. Use a sharp knife to make a shallow, vertical incision in the bark, and use this to grip the top layer of bark and peel it away carefully. Keep these sheets intact as much as possible, and package carefully before returning home so that the bark doesn't crumble en route.

2 Once home, use soap and a sponge to scrub the bark, removing any lichen, moss, or dirt. Examine the bark and trim away any dense, woody edges. Soak the bark in a stock pot of warm water overnight until softened.

3 Once softened, examine the edges of the bark and begin to carefully peel away the individual bark layers. These sheets will be thin and delicate when damp, so work slowly and carefully, as tears cannot be repaired. Rinse any film or chalky sap from these layers, and layer them between sheets of paper towel to dry.

4 To keep the birch paper flat, dry them underneath drying weights or a heavy book.

5 Once dry, the birch paper can be trimmed to even squares and used like any other paper.

SCULPTING WITH PAPER CLAY

When I first started making my own paper, I was rather surprised by the process. When you're used to uniform, machine-processed paper like we are in the modern world, paper almost appears to be a perfect slice of something solid, resembling nothing in the natural world. When I began to make paper myself, I experienced with awe the way these perfect sheets arose from such formlessness. Working with natural fibres always explores this liminal ground between the formed and the formless, encouraging us to break down the structure of the natural world and reimagine it for ourselves. Now that our chapter has explored numerous methods of crafting paper, it's time to remove the last of the constraints from our creative process and bring our work with plant fibres into the third dimension.

Paper clay is a fabulous method of working plant fibres into three-dimensional sculptures, and can be used to craft altarwares and ritual tools using the techniques in this chapter. For this recipe, any combination of paper scraps, plant fibres, and recycled paper will do, so long as it is evenly blended and smooth. While paper clay is not water- or fire-tolerant even when dry, it can still be used to craft a wide variety of magical objects – candle holders, reliquaries, statuary, icons, and altar bowls, to name a few.

Makes: about 900g/2lb paper clay
Prep time: 20 minutes, plus sculpting and drying

FOR THE PAPER

* 60g/2¼oz/½ cup plain/all-purpose flour
* 25g/1oz/¼ cup cornflour/cornstarch
* 1 tablespoon salt
* 250ml/9fl oz/1 cup water
* 2 tablespoons vegetable oil
* Small saucepan
* 500g/1lb 2oz paper or plant fibre pulp, damp but not wet
* Sponge
* Moulds (optional)
* Paint or resin (optional)

1 Mix the flour, cornstarch, and salt in a small bowl. Add the water and vegetable oil, then whisk until evenly combined. There should be no lumps of flour or starch remaining.

2 Place this mixture in your saucepan and stir over a low heat until the liquid thickens to form a "glue" with the consistency of a custard.

3 Put the paper or plant pulp into a larger bowl, pour over the glue, then knead until combined to form a dough. Make sure no lumps of paper pulp remain and the dough is smooth. If the dough is still too sticky, add a small amount of flour or cornflour and knead until combined.

4 This paper clay can be stored in the refrigerator in an airtight container or cling film/plastic wrap for up to 1 week, or in the freezer for up to 3 months. Clay made in advance may need to be refreshed with water once thawed, which can be kneaded into the dough until it is workable again.

5 To sculpt, use as you would any other clay or play dough for hand building. As with mineral clay, use a wet sponge to soften hard edges, or use moulds to form more complex shapes. Allow these forms to dry at room temperature for at least 1 week before use.

6 Your sculptures can be used just as they are, painted, or coated with resin to preserve them. They will keep for years to come, but may become damaged when wet. Clean with a dry or slightly damp towel, never with water.

HAND-BINDING PAPER JOURNALS

It's been said before, but books really are magic. The recording of knowledge in the form of writing is how we time-travel most effectively, inheriting knowledge from writers of the past. Books can be a portal to a particular time and culture, to the mind of an expert, or to the imagination of an artist. While this writing was originally preserved on clay tablets when human languages were forming, history has overwhelmingly preferred plant-based writing materia, like papyrus, parchment, and paper. For witches, this practice gains a deeper meaning, with plants positioned as the keepers of our history and ancestral wisdom. Without these fibre-rich allies to form our books and grimoires, which have allowed humans to share information between centuries and generations, who could say what swerve the fate of humankind may have taken? The world we know today is due in large part to the work of bookmaking and recorded writing, which has only been made possible through the incredible power of plants.

Now that you have mastered the papermaking techniques within this chapter, the final step is learning how to to bind your own handmade books, for use as journals, magical grimoires, Tarot notes, or for recording your dreams. This entry offers some simple steps for hand-binding these small books with thread, but it also shares a short ritual for weaving a little knot magic into our books. Drawing on the inspiration from the book blessings and curses of the Middle Ages, I encourage you to craft a short statement of intent meant to protect yourself, your book, and the hidden secrets within from harm. You may elect to issue a curse, like the 14th-century inscription, "May the one who takes you in theft, by the sword of a demon be cleft", or a blessing, such as, "May the one who carries this book be safe from all harm". Repeat this charm aloud each time you tie the thread or pass the needle through your binding, weaving the consecration into the spine of the book itself.

Prep time: 30 minutes

FOR THE PAPER
* Sheets of handmade paper
* Binder clips
* Thumbtack, awl, or pin
* Needle and thread

1 Lay your sheets of paper down on a flat surface. Use binder clips along the edges of your paper to ensure the pages lie flat and even.

2 Along the centre of the pages, what will be the spine of the book, make 5–6 evenly spaced holes through all pages with a thumbtack, awl, or pin.

3 Thread your needle, but do not tie a knot. Instead, pass the needle through the centermost hole in your book and pull it almost all the way through, leaving a 8cm/3in tail dangling from the end of your thread. Hold this tail in place and continue threading the holes of the binding up to the top edge of the book, passing through each hole. When you reach the top, sew down to the bottom edge of the book, sewing back through your last few stitches. Finally, sew back up to the centre. There should be thread running along both the inner and outer spine of the book. When you reach the centre, tightly tie off your thread using the tail you left at the start of the project.

4 Crease your book along the centre fold and use heavy objects to weigh it down until the paper stays flat.

Candles

Candles

s there a more iconic tool in the witch's cabinet than a candle? A humble vessel for flickering flames, candles symbolize the fire of spirit in so many cultures, allowing us to contain the destructive power of fire safely in our homes. It's important to remember that candles were a necessity for most people throughout history, allowing them to navigate the shadowed world after sundown. As witches of folklore are known for their nocturnal habits, the candle has become a treasured symbol of their nighttime rites, allowing them to work in secret under the cover of darkness. Candles light the altar, call forth the dead, deliver prophecy in mysterious shadows, and glow from atop the witch's stang. We find associations between candles or lamps and magic in even the earliest human civilizations, making these among the earliest forms of magical tech to be developed by ancient witches.

However, candles as we recognize them today would not have been in use until the Roman era, and modern candle magic wouldn't arrive until much later. Before this time, oil lamps would have been the magician's preferred tool, and ancient magic offers many examples of lamp-specific charms and spells, such that lamp magic could be an entire study unto itself. Ancient Egyptian culture did invent a quasi-candle, the rushlight, made from dried rushes soaked in melted animal fats, but lamps were far more easily available and durable, and thus took precedence in homes and temples. Ancient Egyptian magicians used these lamps in dream incubation rituals, retreating into south-facing caves and watching gentle lamp flames as they fell into a deep trance. Diyas, or small lamps fuelled with clarified butter, have been common in Hindu and Buddhist celebrations for thousands of years, specifically in honour of the Hindu goddess Lakshmi at the festival of Diwali, where the diyas represent a triumph of light over darkness. In Ancient Greek magic, lamps of this type were often used in this form of divination, as well as in creating powerful, malicious love charms. In the Zoroastrian faith, all forms of light and fire are held in such reverence that it is considered unlucky and taboo to blow out a candle with one's breath, a tradition still practised by many modern witches today. While magic lamps have fallen out of prominence over the millennia since these spells were written, lamp magic is the predecessor of the candle magic we know today, and speaks to an ancient insistence upon the power of magic worked by fire.

When candles did arrive, around 1000–500 BCE, they were not the fragrant boutique candles that you and I are used to in the modern world. These early tapers were made of hard animal fats like beef tallow and whale blubber, and gave off foul aromas when burned. Luckily, the use of beeswax soon followed, as this wax produces candles that hold their shape and cast very little fragrance. While this wax was, until the early modern period, quite a costly luxury item, beeswax candles were so highly prized that it is Christian tradition for the Pascal candle, burned on Easter Sunday, to be made of solid beeswax. *The Malleus Maleficarum*,[x] the premier witch-hunting manual of the 1400s, lists consecrated church candles like these as being among the foremost tools that can be used "for preserving oneself from the injury of witches". This same book cites candles as being central to the sabbatic rites of witches, where they steal away to the woods and light their ritual candles from the one which burns between the Devil's horns.

Once candles became more commonplace in Europe, they featured much more prominently in spell books and magical operations. Divination by wax, or ceromancy, became more popular as a result, as well as capnomancy, or smoke divination, from the snuffing of candle flames. Most famously the *Petit Albert*,[xi] an 18th-century French grimoire, outlines a procedure for making the Hand of Glory, a pickled hand of a malefactor which, when used as a candle stick to hold a magic candle, will unlock any door and render motionless all who behold it. The same book outlined procedures for making candles out of human fat, which would crackle and sparkle to reveal the locations of hidden treasure. In *Three Books of Occult Philosophy*, Agrippa makes note of several candle and lamp charms, including producing apparitions by candles, such that burning oil into which grape flowers have been infused should produce a vision of grapes in the lamp light. He also mentions that all fires can be used to cast away evil spirits, and that malevolent spirits thrive in darkness, while helpful guides and angels are aided by light, therefore insisting that "worships whatsoever

should not be performed without lighted candles".

In modern magic, candles still hold a central role in spellcraft, and are considered by many to represent their own school of magical arte. Many modern practitioners claim to specialize in candle magic, which typically involves carving candles with wax sigils and dressing them in herbs and oils, before surrounding them with sympathetic materia and burning them to completion. This modern practice places additional emphasis on candle colours, which is rarely seen in magical history. Here, colours associated with specific aims – green for money, red for love, etc. – are present in pigmented waxes, adding a dose of colour magic to the witch's rites. Other practitioners, especially those operating within hoodoo and rootwork traditions, hollow out the bases of their candles to insert "charges", or collections of herbs, dirts, powders, and petitions, which will catch fire as the candle burns and be sublimated with the wax. Even simple blessings upon candles to give them over to a spiritual purpose, seen so often in Catholic folk magic, can be enough to transform these simple forms of wax and wick into indispensable magical tools.

In my own practice, candles are used to light altars to spirits when congress is sought, or offerings are given. I light candles on my ancestral altar regularly, as a method of caring for my beloved dead, and keeping our relationship alive. I also save the spilled wax of previous candles, especially those used for spellwork, and melt them down

again to create altar lights, which allow me to read from my spellbooks in darkness. One of my favourite personal rituals involves blessing beeswax candles on the winter solstice, to be used in rites of chasing away the ghosts of winter and cultivating light and warmth within the season of darkness. These tapers are carved with sigils representing my personal craft, powdered with freshly scraped nutmeg (a favourite herb of St Hildegard von Bingen for keeping a joyful heart), sprinkled with evergreen tea (a perennial symbol of triumph over death), passed through the smoke of frankincense (an exorcism herb of the sun), and burned after sundown on days when the darkness of winter is too deep to bear. This small and humble rite makes a great coven craft for the shortest day of the year, and calls upon traditional folklore around this holiday for generating light, hope, and faith as countermeasures toward the malevolence of winter.

In the following pages, you will be guided through a number of techniques for crafting magical candles – pouring them, dipping them, moulding them, and even extracting your own wax from natural bayberries. Some of these recipes have their own magical history, like the Mullein Torch Tapers, but many do not, inviting you to bring the trappings of your own practice to the crafting process. There is a reason my shop only sells blank candles – the magic really begins when we customize these works for our intentions and aims. Using the simple structures ahead, experiment with carving and dressing these candles to your heart's content, tapping into your soulful, creative fire as you take up the tools of wax and wick.

Candlemaking tools

In order to proceed with the recipes ahead, there are a few key pieces of equipment that will be necessary to have on hand. Since making candles requires working with hot waxes, using proper tools like these can help us work neatly and safely.

* **WAX MELTING POT** – These are often tall handled vessels with a pour spout, sold specifically for working with wax in candlemaking. However, you can create your own in a pinch from any tall, sturdy container made from metal or heatproof glass.

* **STOCK POT** – The waxes in this chapter are melted using a bain-marie, or the double boiler method. In this case, wax melting pots or heating vessels are submerged into a stock pot of simmering water, allowing the wax to melt without overheating. No matter what recipe you use, you will need to have a stock pot that can comfortably fit your wax melting vessel.

* **OVEN MITTS/HEATPROOF GLOVES** – These are helpful to have on hand for moving and handling hot vessels, pots, and equipment. While you may not need them for every craft, keep them nearby in case to prevent accidental burns.

* **THERMOMETER** – The recipes ahead require us to heat wax, fragrances, and pigments to specific temperatures to deliver the best results. Any thermometer you want to use is fine, but as wax is very difficult to clean, simple stick thermometers or no-contact laser thermometers may be preferable.

- **GREASEPROOF/WAX PAPER & TINFOIL** – Dripping and spilling wax is an unavoidable part of the candlemaking process, so covering our work surfaces will protect against waste and damage. You may use whatever workspace cover you like, but the benefit of using a non-stick surface like greaseproof paper or foil is that any spilled wax can be allowed to cool and then peeled away easily for remelting.

- **FRAGRANCES & PIGMENTS** – The recipes ahead leave lots of room for customization. If you choose to add fragrance or colour to your candles, make sure that these are oil or powder-based compounds, as water-based fragrances and colours will not mix with waxes.

With this information in mind, you're ready to begin your candlemaking journey. Below you will find some general steps and the overview of the process for making candles, along with some useful tips and techniques. These steps provide a very loose outline of the process, and the recipes ahead in this chapter will give further details on the procedures for specific candle crafts. However, a quick overview of candle science and chemistry may still be helpful in your crafting, especially in making discernments between different types of waxes and wicks. These simple, structural elements can make the difference between a candle that works and a candle that doesn't. If you've ever had your candle wicks drown themselves in wax, tunnel through the centre of the candle, or burn so hot they shatter glass containers, these problems can be solved and avoided by making proper selections of materia and tools in our crafting process. Please read these steps carefully before proceeding.

How to make candles
STEP 1 –
Choose your wax

Waxes are used as fuel for our candles, but not all waxes are created equal, and choosing the right wax for your candle could be the difference between success and disaster. The most common waxes you'll find in candlemaking are soy wax, palm wax, paraffin, coconut wax, rapeseed wax, and beeswax. In the same way that plant oils come with different viscosities and textures (consider the difference between slick olive oil and solid coconut oil), waxes also come in varying degrees of hardness. For example, soy wax tends to be quite soft, while beeswax is among the hardest waxes. As a general rule, harder waxes will burn hotter, which is why beeswax is usually poured into metal containers rather than glass ones. Soy wax, on the other hand, melts at a low enough temperature that it is often used for massage candles, meant to be dripped directly onto the skin. This could never be done with beeswax, and anyone who has ever accidentally dripped a beeswax candle on their hand knows why! Consider the melting temperatures in the table on page 149 for some useful information that will help you choose the right wax.

Because many commercially available waxes are often heavily refined from their natural sources, choosing our wax also raises a question here about ecological sustainability. Overall, beeswax generally has the lowest environmental impact, because it comes from a completely renewable source. Paraffin wax, on the other hand, is derived from petroleum, when crude oil is dewaxed and purified, making this the least sustainable option. Soy and palm waxes fall somewhere in the middle, being from renewable plant-based

sources, but also supporting the palm and soy industries, which are major contributors to global deforestation. While coconut and rapeseed waxes are slowly emerging as more eco-friendly alternatives , these are still on the high end of the price spectrum, making them inaccessible to many.

STEP 2 –
Select your candle wicks

Wicks may seem a cursory addition to the candlemaking process, but they are essential. A poorly structured wick can make hours of candlemaking redundant. The purpose of these little strings and slivers of wood is to soak up the melting wax or "fuel" of our candle, and burn it effectively at a rate that allows the candle to burn to completion. Thin, stringy wicks will burn down before the candle is through, and thick wicks will burn the candle too quickly, drowning themselves in the wax or struggling to stay aflame. In general, braided cotton cordage seems to be the best and most used fibre wicking on the market, with absorbent softwoods, like maple, birch, or rosewood, being the best choices for wooden wicks.

There is also something to be said for the placement of our wicks within the candles. This is most important for poured candles, as moulded shapes or slender tapers are often too thin to support multiple flames without melting too quickly. As a general rule, use one wick for every 8cm/3in-wide candle, and an additional wick for every 2cm/1in thereafter. A 10cm/4in-wide candle will need two wicks, a 12cm/5in-wide candle will need three wicks, and so on. Without these additional wicks, much of the candle wax will go to waste, sticking to the sides of the candle vessel, too far from the flame to melt.

STEP 3 –
Melt your waxes

No matter what kind of candle you're trying to make, melting your wax is where the work truly begins. However, this process is not as simple as it looks. Overheating our wax can lead to changes in wax texture, yielding suboptimal results in our finished products. For this reason, it's important to heat our waxes gently using a double boiler or wax melter, which ensures the temperature of our melted wax will stay consistent.

Temperatures are not only important for melting our wax, but also for pouring our candles, and adding fragrance and pigment to the wax base. If you are adding pigment to your candles, do this when the wax is at its hottest, while still in the bain-marie/double boiler, to ensure it is fully incorporated. If you are adding fragrance, this should also be done when the wax is hot enough for the fragrance to bind to the wax molecules. This will ensure your fragrance has good "throw", meaning it carries well throughout a room while the candle burns. You can find further details about adding fragrance and colour in the recipes ahead, but the cart opposite should be a handy guide in navigating the particulars of heating, pouring, and cooling whatever wax you choose to work with.

STEP 4 –
Cure and burn your candle

It's important to note that all these waxes benefit from a curing period after pouring. While firm waxes can appear to set completely within minutes, a complete cooldown and a few days of setting time will improve burnability of your candles, preventing tunnelling (the candle burns

Wax	Melting temperature	Fragrance adding temperature	Pouring temperature
Beeswax	63°C/145°F	85°C/185°F	68°C/155°F
Palm wax	71°C/160°F	82°C/180°F	93°C/200°F
Soy wax	52°C/125°F	82°C/180°F	57°C/135°F
Coconut wax	40°C/105°F	85°C/185°F	88°C/190°F
Rapeseed wax	82°C/180°F	70°C/158°F	77°C/170°F
Paraffin wax	52°C/125°F	93°C/200°F	77°C/170°F

only through the centre of the wax, leaving a ring of untouched wax around the edge of the candle) and ensuring the best throw of your fragrance. Hard waxes like beeswax and paraffin only need a few days of curing, while softer waxes like soy wax will continue to harden and set for weeks after pouring. As a general rule, I like to give all candles, of any wax type, a curing period of seven days before burning. This compensates for seasonal changes (warmer weather means slower cure times) and works as a good median cure time between all wax types.

While the process for creating different types of candles will vary, this general guide will help get you started, and further detail on procedure can be explored in the recipes ahead. Some of these will feature interesting historical flames that are very different from our modern conception of what a candle should be, like the Mullein Torch Tapers (see page 161) or Edible Butter Candles (see page 162). These should hopefully broaden your own ideas of magical candlework and encourage you to get as creative as you possibly can. Remember, in both magic and art, acts of creation are always governed by the element of fire.

POURED CANDLES

Pouring wax is one of the simplest methods for beginner candlemakers to master. It requires just three ingredients – wax, wick, and vessel – allowing you to be creative while honing your skills with fragrance and pigments. This is also the candlemaking method with the fewest steps, requiring much more patience and fewer active steps than other styles of candlecraft. Additionally, poured candles can be made with any wax you have on hand, and are an excellent way to upcycle old jam jars, teacups, and other containers. Just be sure to use vessels made of heatproof materials, like metal, glass, or ceramic.

You may be tempted to top your poured candles with leaves, flowers, and pressed herbs to give your candles an extra "boost" of magic . While this certainly adds a decorative finish, it presents a worrisome fire hazard, especially if using dried plants. If you are hesitant to leave your candles bare, consider non-combustible alternatives like crystals or wax flowers, avoiding dried flowers, resins, and plastics. For an added layer of fire safety, burn all poured candles on top of heatproof surfaces like ceramic or glass, especially once the candle is near its end.

Prep time: 45 minutes, plus cooling and 1 week curing

FOR THE CANDLE
* 900g/2lb candle wax (see pages 146–8)
* Wax heating vessel
* Stock pot
* Candle vessels
* Cotton wicks
* Wick holders
* Fragrance/pigments (optional)
* Thermometer
* Greaseproof/wax paper/tinfoil

I Place your wax in the heating vessel and set this into your stock pot. Fill the stock pot with water and bring to the boil, creating a bain-marie. Melt your wax completely according to the temperatures given on page 149.

2 While the wax melts, prepare your candle vessels with wicks and wick holders. Make sure that these wicks are secure and placed exactly where you like.

3 If you are adding fragrance or pigments to your wax, consult the temperature chart on page 149 to determine when to make these additions.

4 When your wax is melted and ready to be poured, take the pot off the heat and remove your wax heating vessel to begin the cooling process. If your vessel does not have a pour spout, transfer the wax to a suitable container at this stage, such as a measuring cup or glass pitcher.

5 Use a thermometer to determine when your wax is at the right pouring temperature (see page 149). If you do not have a thermometer handy, you should pour the wax just when it begins to become opaque. If your work room is very cold, you might want to pour your wax at a slightly higher temperature, when the wax is not yet opaque but the outside of your pouring vessel is just cool enough to touch.

6 While you wait for the wax to cool, line your workstation with greaseproof paper or tinfoil and set your candle vessels on top.

7 Pour your wax into the candle vessels, making sure not to jostle your wick holders as you work. Be sure to leave a few millimeters of space at the top of the vessel, so you don't accidentally overpour.

8 When all candles are poured, allow them to cool at room temperature until fully set, at least 1 hour.

9 Once set, trim your wicks, remove the wick holders, and cure your candles for an additional week before burning. This is an especially important step for poured candles, and for those working with softer waxes like soy and coconut. It will improve both burnability and scent throw of your candles, leading to a noticeably finer product.

DIPPED CANDLES

Candle dipping is the traditional method of making candlesticks and tapers. This method traces its origins back to the Roman era, when crafters used tallow, a waxy substance made from rendered animal fat, to produce candles cheaply for a wide audience. While this method is slow and labour-intensive, traditional candle-dipping factories created elaborate rigs, attaching wicks to marionette-like beams and dipping large amounts of candles (sometimes over 50 at once!) into big vats of melted wax. This process was popular in monasteries and convents of the Middle Ages, which produced candles in great numbers for spiritual services and for sale. Using the same basic methods as the Ancient Romans, our candle-dipping procedure in this chapter works in a much smaller batch, but yields the same finished product with a delightful handmade touch that will not be found with other candlemaking methods.

This process requires some additional equipment and considerations that other methods do not. First, dipped candles need a very deep wax heating vessel – deep enough for the length of candle you wish to create. If you do not have a tall melting pot handy, a clean repurposed glass votive jar or tall, wide-mouthed Mason jar will work in a pinch. However, it is important to note that some waxes, like beeswax or paraffin, have high melting points and can become so hot that they can shatter glass; in these cases, it is best to use a metal melting pot. Additionally, this method will require more wax than other methods, as the melted wax needs to fill our melting vessel almost to the rim, so that when our wicks are dipped, they are fully coated. Our wicks will also differ here. Other recipes use single wicks with a metal tab at the base for attaching to a vessel surface, while dipped candles use lengths of the same cotton wicking cord with no metal bases. Finally, if you are using a softer wax like coconut or soy, you may get better results from allowing your candles to cool completely in a bucket of cold water in between dippings; you may end up working longer and harder if you skip this step. This is not so necessary for harder waxes, like beeswax, paraffin, or rapeseed.

If you want to dip more candles at once, consider using an X-shaped bracket or two dowels tied together at the centre to dip up to eight candles at a time, with each wick looped over one end of the X. You will need a wider dipping vessel for this, but this small investment in equipment will greatly speed up your production, allowing you to follow in the footsteps of historical candlemakers and make this slow, laborious process as efficient as possible.

Recipe continues overleaf

Prep time: 1 hour, plus cooling and 1 week curing

FOR THE CANDLE

* Cotton wicking cord
* Candle weights or 4 coins
* 1.3kg/3lb candle wax (beeswax works best)
* Wax heating vessel
* Stock pot
* Fragrance/pigments (optional)
* Thermometer
* Deep bucket of cool water (optional)
* Broomstick or other drying pole

I Take a piece of cotton wicking cord, about 60cm/2ft in length, and place a weight on each end. Each length of wick will create two candles. If you do not have candle weights at home, you can use metal coins instead by placing a small drop of melted wax at each end of the wick and sandwiching two coins around it, sealing them together.

2 Place your wax in the heating vessel and set this into your stock pot. Fill the stock pot with water and bring to the boil, creating a bain-marie. Melt your wax completely, ensuring it is deep enough for you to dip your candles to the desired length.

3 If you are adding fragrance or pigment to your wax, consult the temperature chart on page 149 to determine when to make these additions.

4 If necessary, set up your bucket of cold water nearby. You will also want to set up a pole to hang your tapers as they dry and set, such as a broomstick placed over two chairs, or a metal hanger suspended from a hook. Even a doorknob will do in a pinch.

5 With your setup complete and your wax fully melted, it's time to get dipping! Hold your wick in the centre with both weights hanging down evenly and plunge these quickly into the wax. Hold them over the pot until they stop dripping, and repeat. You may dip up to 3 times, and then allow your candles to cool on your drying pole for about 5 minutes, or plunge them into cold water to speed up the process.

6 When your candles are about 1.5cm/½in wide, trim off the weights and peel them out of the wax. This wax can be remelted in the pot, and fresh wax can always be added if you see that the pot is running low; just be sure to adjust your fragrance and/or pigment if necessary.

7 Repeat the dipping process until your candle is the desired thickness.

8 When completed, allow your candles to hang over the drying pole overnight to firm up, then trim the wicks in the morning. Like all candles, these benefit from a 1-week curing process before burning. This step is not necessary, but greatly improves the fragrance and burnability of your tapers.

MOULDED CANDLES

Moulded candles are quite dramatic to behold but creating them at home is fairly simple. These candles are the sculptural cousin of poured candles, relying on many similar techniques but using decorative moulds to achieve a finished product that is both free-standing and full of character. These can be in any shape you wish, from pillars to Greek statues, and present a simpler, faster alternative for making tapers than the traditional dipping method. Moulds can also be used again and again, enabling candlemakers to achieve precise copies of their candle shapes.

While there are many benefits to moulding candles, there is however one significant downside: not all shapes were meant to be candles, and some moulds for wider, deeper forms yield mixed results. As the wick burns, it will bore a hole through the centre of any shape that is too wide, leaving you with lots of misshapen, half-melted wax once the candle expires. Savvy crafters can work around this by using multiple wicks, or choosing moulds for slimmer, more elegant shapes. In general, for a free-standing form, one standard cotton wick will melt wax within a 8cm/3in radius. Keep this ratio in mind as you choose your moulds, or plan to reuse whatever wax may be left over after the burn.

Additionally, care should be taken when choosing the type of wax used for moulded candles. Softer waxes, like soy and coconut, may not unmould properly, or may adhere to the sides of a mould and be difficult to remove. There is nothing worse than spending hours melting and pouring wax only to mangle it while trying to remove it from a mould! Some companies do maker firmer soy and coconut waxes, usually called "pillar" wax, but using hard waxes like beeswax, paraffin, or rapeseed will remove all guesswork from your process.

Silicone, metal, and hard acrylic moulds exist, with acrylic and metal being slightly more difficult to use but leading to a finer product with more clearly defined edges. Acrylic and metal moulds are also more durable and affordable, meaning candlemakers will be able to get more use out of them.

Prep time: 45 minutes, plus cooling and 1 week curing

FOR THE CANDLE

* 900g/2lb hard candle wax (beeswax, paraffin, or rapeseed)
* Wax heating vessel
* Stock pot
* Cotton wicks
* Wick holder or bobby pin
* Candle mould (hard acrylic, metal, or silicone)
* Rubber mould plug or small strip of duct tape
* Fragrances/pigments (optional)
* Thermometer
* Greaseproof/wax paper or tinfoil

1 Place your wax in the heating vessel and set this into your stock pot. Fill the stock pot with water and bring to the boil, creating a bain-marie. Melt your wax completely according to the temperatures given on page 149.

2 While the wax melts, prepare your candle vessels with wicks and wick holders. Thread the wick through the mould, then plug the bottom wick opening with either a rubber plug or a small strip of duct tape. If using tape, make sure to get a good, strong seal before proceeding. You can test this by pouring a bit of hot water into the mould and checking for any drips. Secure the upper part of the wick with a wick holder or bobby pin, or if the opening is larger, two bamboo skewers clamped together around the wick to hold it in place. Acrylic and metal moulds sometimes benefit from a quick spritz of non-stick cooking spray, which will help you unmould later.

3 If you are adding fragrance or pigments to your wax, consult the temperature chart on page 149 to determine when to make these additions.

Recipe continues overleaf

4 When your wax is melted and ready to be poured, take the pot off the heat and remove your wax heating vessel to begin the cooling process. If your vessel does not have a pour spout, transfer the wax to a suitable container at this stage, such as a measuring cup or glass pitcher.

5 Use a thermometer to determine when your wax is at the right pouring temperature (see page 149). If you do not have a thermometer handy, you should pour the wax just when it begins to become opaque. If your work room is very cold, you might want to pour your wax at a slightly higher temperature, when the wax is not yet opaque but the outside of your pouring vessel is just cool enough to touch.

6 While you wait for the wax to cool, line your workstation with greaseproof paper or tinfoil and set your candle vessels on top.

7 Fill your moulds to the desired height, then allow them to cool until solid at room temperature. If necessary, you may need to top off the moulds with wax as they set, as some waxes will leave an undesirable dimple or pit near the wick, making your candles unstable when unmoulded.

8 Once poured and fully set, transfer your moulds to the refrigerator or freezer for 1 hour before unmoulding.

9 To unmould, remove your candle from the refrigerator or freezer. For silicone moulds, gently loosen the mould from the wax, working from the top downwards, until the entire candle comes free. For metal or acrylic moulds, gently tap the candle on a hard surface to loosen it and pull it out neatly from the mould. If it is stubborn, you can run the mould under warm water until the candle springs free. Allow these candles to cure at room temperature for 1 week before burning.

SCENTED CANDLES

There is no room or setting which could not be in some way improved by the presence of a scented candle. The flickering flame coupled with a delicious fragrance is one of the most relaxing things in the world. Adding fragrance to our candles is a very simple process, and can be applied to any wax or candlemaking method. However, there are a few important points to take note of before beginning your own scented candle journey.

Firstly, selecting a fragrance is of the utmost importance. Since wax is hydrophobic, meaning it does not mix with watery substances, only oil-based fragrances should be used to make candles. For those seeking a natural approach, essential oils are an obvious choice. However, these are often quite costly to purchase in the quantities required for candlemaking, and since candles are not for internal use of any kind, high-quality, naturally derived fragrance oils are a more affordable alternative.

Savvy candlemakers will take a few notes from perfumers in blending the ideal ratio of fragrances. If you are using more than one fragrance in your blend, consider including a mix of head, heart, and base notes to make the finished product more harmonious. Head notes are the most delicate, referring to scents which are crisp, refreshing, and sharp, like light florals or citrus. Heart notes are the core of your blend, and feature spicy, rounded, and balanced scents like bold florals and spices. Base notes, used very sparingly, make up the velvety underpinning of your scent, and are typically woody, resinous, smoky, and deep. Base and head notes should be used sparingly, with heart notes making up the bulk of your blend. When used in proper ratios, these scents enhance one another, like the notes that make up a musical chord.

Additionally, being mindful of our wax temperatures is key to developing a good scented candle. Wax usually melts at a high temperature, which is hot enough to distort, mutate, and even ignite our fragrances. While adding fragrance to wax will often make it more stable and insulated from the destructive power of heat, repeated cooling and heating cycles can make our fragrances change, become acrid, or dissipate altogether. Because of this, fragrance oils must also be added to the wax at the appropriate temperature and then poured immediately. This ensures that the wax and fragrance are chemically bonded, and produces a stronger "throw", or the reach of a fragrance within a room. Please refer to the table given earlier in this chapter (see page 149) for a list of common waxes and their ideal fragrance mixing temperatures, and use a wax thermometer to determine the precise moment for mixing your scented candles. As a general rule, for 450g/1lb of wax, 30ml/1fl oz of fragrance oil is typically sufficient.

Prep time: 45 minutes, plus cooling and 1 week curing

FOR THE CANDLE
* 900g/2lb candle wax
* Wax heating vessel
* Stock pot
* Candle vessels
* Cotton wicking cord
* Wick holders
* Greaseproof/wax paper/tinfoil
* Oil-based fragrance

I Place your wax in the heating vessel and set this into your stock pot. Fill the stock pot with water and bring to the boil, creating a bain-marie. Melt your wax completely according to the temperatures given on page 149.

2 While the wax melts, prepare your candle vessels with wicks and wick holders. Make sure that these wicks are secure and placed exactly where you like. Set these vessels onto a prepared, covered workspace.

3 Use a thermometer to heat the wax to the ideal temperature for adding fragrance. Carefully measure your fragrance, and add this to the melted wax, stirring for at least 1 full minute in order to thoroughly combine.

4 Remove the wax from the heat, and allow to cool to the ideal pouring temperature for your wax. Pour all the wax you created, as scented wax should not be reheated and poured again.

5 Allow these candles to cool completely, then cure for at least 1 week for best results.

NATURALLY COLOURED CANDLES

Witches are familiar with the importance of candle colours. Red candles are used for love magic, green for drawing money, black for banishing and cursing, etc. This tradition is relatively modern, with coloured candles gaining mass-market popularity in the 18th and 19th centuries. These modern candle colours, sold as micas, oxides, dyes, and lake pigments, make it easy for contemporary practitioners to extract colour into their wax, giving us the bold colours we see today.

However, not all powdered pigments are suitable for candle crafting. As candle wicks work through capillary action, absorbing wax as fuel, insoluble powdered pigments will clog the wick. Water- or alcohol-based dyes will not emulsify, leading to beads of colour sunk to the bottom. Luckily, common herbs and spices, like turmeric, paprika, or wheatgrass provide beautiful colours. These pigments take much longer to infuse (over 24 hours), but give candlemakers a natural alternative to processed chemical wax dyes and micas.

These plant pigments may express their colours differently in wax than on fabric or paper. For example, wheatgrass powder produces a bright green in candles, but will dye a deep olive or brown on fabrics. You also need to keep in mind that waxes have natural colours that may interfere with your pigments. Beeswax is a luscious golden yellow even after dyed. Soy wax tends toward the paler side, with pigments becoming more pastel when infused. These dye herbs also have their own fragrances, so make sure to choose a fragrance for your candle that is harmonious with its scent.

Prep time: 24 hours, plus cooling

FOR THE CANDLE

* 900g/1lb candle wax
* Wax heating vessel
* Stock pot
* 3–5 tablespoons pigmented herb powder
* Coffee filter
* Short length of string or rubber band

1 Place your wax in the heating vessel and set this into your stock pot. Fill the stock pot with water and bring to the boil, creating a bain-marie. Melt your wax completely according to the temperatures given on page 149.

2 Place the powdered pigment into a coffee filter. Tie this filter into a pouch using string or a rubber band, and gently submerge it in the wax until fully saturated.

3 Keep your heat low while still maintaining the proper wax temperature. Allow these herbs to slowly infuse over the course of 24 hours, keeping an eye on your hob/stove and testing the wax occasionally to see how well the colours are coming along. If you find after 4–8 hours that your colours are not as strong as you would like, consider adding a second dye pouch to the wax, containing more of the pigment, and make a note for yourself about the amount used for further candlemaking experiments.

4 After 24 hours of infusion, once you have achieved your desired result gently remove the dye pouch from the wax. Press this against the side of your wax heating vessel to extract all the liquid before discarding. This coloured wax can be used immediately or cooled to save for future projects.

Candle dye herbs

Alkanet – deep burgundy red	**Nettle** – light olive
Annato – yellow	**Paprika** – vibrant orange
Beetroot powder – deep red/purple	**Peppermint** – light green
Charcoal – black	**Red clay** – brick red
Cinnamon – warm brown	**Rosehip powder** – reddish orange
Clove – deep brown	**Saffron** – golden yellow
Comfrey – bright green	**Spirulina** – warm, brownish green
Madder root – peach or orange	**Turmeric** – bright orange or yellow
Matcha – earthy green	**Wheatgrass powder** – bright green

MULLEIN TORCH TAPERS

Mullein is a fabulous medicinal and garden herb with soft, velvety leaves and towering stalks of flowers. It is an anti-inflammatory herb, particularly for the lungs, and is often used in herbal medicine to treat coughs and asthma. Both the leaves and the stalks of these plants have been used in candlemaking since Ancient Greece and Rome, earning mullein the folk names "candlewick" and "hag's taper". Ancient peoples dipped the dried stalks or rolled dried leaves in wax, and found that these densely fibrous plants burn surprisingly well as wicks and torches.

In modern practice, these are a sustainable alternative to normal candlesticks. Since mullein is tenaciously invasive, harvesting these plants can be helpful for our local environment. Even if it is not invasive, this plant is highly abundant, making it safe to harvest in autumn. These tapers burn faster than regular candlesticks, and produce a wider, torch-like flame. The seeds snap and crackle as they burn, producing a comforting sound similar to a campfire. Often associated with necromancy and the spirits of the dead, these candles are typically reserved for special occasions, such as Samhain. These associations have given mullein tapers an additional folk name: "corpse candles". Mullein is correspondent with the planet Saturn, so these can be used for all Saturnine magics, like hexes and maledictions, as well as work with spirits of the dead, chthonic deities, or in funerary rites.

Prep time: 30–45 minutes, plus cooling and 1 week curing

FOR THE CANDLE

* Dried mullein stalks, no thicker than ½cm/1in at the widest
* At least 900g/2lb candle wax (beeswax works best)
* Wax heating vessel
* Stock pot
* Bamboo skewers (optional)
* Greaseproof/wax paper

I Trim your mullein stalks to lengths that can be completely submerged within your wax heating vessel. If you want to make your candles free-standing, make sure they have a flat base. You may wish to leave a small bit of stem at the end of your stalks to hold as you dip them, or pierce the centre of the stalk with a bamboo skewer to hold them. Do not attempt to use your fingertips to dip the mullein stalks into the wax, as it can get quite hot when melted and can cause burns.

2 It is important to have enough wax on hand to fill your wax heating vessel at least 1.5 times, as these torches soak up a lot of wax during the crafting process. Thicker stalks will use more wax. If you notice the level of wax getting low, simply add more to bring it back to the correct depth.

3 Place your wax in the heating vessel and set this into your stock pot. Fill the stock pot with water and bring to the boil, creating a bain-marie. Melt your wax completely according to the temperatures given on page 149.

4 When the wax is melted and your stalks are cut and prepared, submerge a stalk fully beneath the wax. You will see air bubbles escaping as wax rushes to fill the empty space. When these bubbles subside, gently lift the stalk out of the wax, and hold it above the melting pot to allow excess wax to drip off.

5 When it stops dripping, transfer the taper to your greaseproof paper to cool for 2 minutes. Some wax will drip out onto the paper, and this can be trimmed with a paring knife once firm and remelted. If you are making free-standing tapers, try to use any excess soft wax to help your candle stand upright; this can be trimmed back later. Repeat this dipping process 5–8 times, or until the stalk has absorbed all that it can and is encased in a thin but visible layer of wax. Be sure to make any final trimmings to the bottom of your taper before the final dip, as this will help round out any uneven edges.

6 Allow these candles to harden at room temperature upon the greaseproof paper, and then cure for 1 week before burning.

7 To burn, place your taper in a candle holder or in a heatproof dish, and use a lighter to gently melt the wax at the tip until the end of the stalk catches fire. They will produce a larger flame and burn quicker than typical candles.

EDIBLE BUTTER CANDLES

While it may sound strange to a modern audience, butter candles are some of the oldest and most traditional candles in history. These trace their earliest origins to the Himalayas, where yak butter was once the candlemaking substance of choice. These simple moulded candles have seen a resurgence in popularity, starring as the unexpected, interactive centerpieces of feast tables, infused with a variety of herbs and spices. As the candle melts, the butter softens like wax, allowing guests to carve away bits of warm, infused butter with their knives, or soak their bread directly in the drippings. While these flavours and seasonings here are just some of my personal favourites, feel free to get as creative as you'd like, tailoring this simple procedure to your favourite flavours and fragrances.

This recipe is perfect for any feast, festival, offering, or decadent dinner, but particularly those that celebrate butter, like Beltane or Maslenitsa. Butter candles are also beautiful offerings to spirits, particularly souls of the dead or beloved ancestors who would have enjoyed this delicacy in life. However, this recipe is also a fine occasion to show off your candlemaking skills, presenting a humble dinnertime staple in a surprising new way for your guests.

Makes: 1 candle

Prep time: 20 minutes, plus chilling

FOR THE CANDLE

* Mixing bowl
* 225g/8oz high-quality butter, softened
* 2 tablespoons finely chopped rosemary
* 1 teaspoon ground white pepper
* 1 tablespoon crushed garlic
* 1 paper cup or candle mould
* Cotton wicking cord
* A small strip of tape
* Wick holder or bobby pin

I In a mixing bowl, stir together your butter and seasonings, and taste-test until everything is just so.

2 Prepare your candle vessel. If you're using a candle mould, prepare this according to the instructions on pages 155–6. If not, use a paper cup to create a squat pillar candle with enough buttery goodness to be dipped and spread for hours. Make a small hole in the bottom of your cup, and thread the wick through it. Seal this hole with a small strip of tape. Suspend your wick across the rim of the cup with a wick holder or bobby pin.

3 Spoon the butter into your mould, tapping against a hard surface to remove any air bubbles along the way. Once your vessel is filled, use a spatula to neatly smooth the bottom of the candle, then transfer to the refrigerator where the candle can set completely.

4 As these candles contain fresh herbs, their shelf life is significantly reduced. Store them for 4–5 days in the refrigerator, or up to 6 weeks in the freezer. When ready to use, remove your candle from the refrigerator and unmould while it is still cold. Place on a small serving dish to catch all drips and dribbles, and serve with bread, or hold the candle and drip the hot herb-infused butter over meats, vegetables, pasta, or anything you wish.

NATURAL BAYBERRY WAX CANDLES

Bayberry candles are a delight and have been resurrected from the annals of history by intrepid herbalists and foragers over the last few decades. Creating these perfumed tapers is a laborious undertaking, as the wax is extracted directly from the wild berries themselves by boiling the fruit until a layer of wax forms on the water's surface. Traditionally, these candles were burned on Christmas or New Year's Eve, to call forth blessings of health, wealth, and happiness in the New Year. These holiday candles were burned one at a time and all the way to completion because they are so precious and difficult to craft. Also called "candleberry", the bayberry has retained the virtues of drawing forth abundance and peace, corresponding with the benevolent planet Jupiter and the fragrance-ruling element of air.

This recipe may sound impractical if you cannot imagine justifying a day of foraging berries and boiling wax for just a few slim taper candles. Bayberry candles are certainly a LOT of work, but this historical recipe gives us deeper insight into the resourcefulness of candlemakers of the past, who used whatever they had on hand to create light within the darkness. There is also nothing like the warm, fruity fragrance of a true bayberry candle, and as the northern bayberry is an invasive plant in many places, harvesting large numbers of bayberries has a positive environmental impact. If you cannot pick your own berries, they can be bought online.

These are dipped candles, as traditional bayberry tapers always are, so be sure to familiarize yourself with the dipped instructions on pages 152–4 first.

Prep time: 3 hours, plus cooling and 1 week curing

FOR THE CANDLE
* 7kg/15lb northern bayberries
* Large stock pot
* Cheesecloth
* Cotton wicking cord
* Candle weights
* 900g/2lb beeswax

1 Place the bayberries in a large stock pot and cover them with water. Bring to the boil and then turn down the heat and briskly simmer the berries for at least 30 minutes.

2 Remove the pot from the heat and strain the berries from the wax. Allow this to stand at room temperature until the wax is fully hardened, then discard the water. You may choose to keep and dry the berries for use in incense and plant magic, as they will still retain their fragrance and magical properties. The collected bayberry wax should weigh close to 450g/1lb.

3 When you are ready to make your candles, prepare the wicks with weights upon the end (see page 154, step 1).

4 Place your bayberry wax and beeswax into the heating vessel and set this into your stock pot. Fill the stock pot with water and bring to the boil, creating a bain-marie. Melt your wax completely according to the temperatures given on page 149. By itself, bayberry wax is on the crumbly side, but when fortified with beeswax it works delightfully with candles and still retains its trademark fragrance.

5 When the waxes are melted, dip your tapers following the method on pages 152–4, and allow them to fully set overnight. As with all candles, these tapers benefit from a 1-week curing process. This is not necessary, but greatly enhances both the fragrance and burnability of the candles. If you are crafting for a holiday celebration, please remember to work ahead of time so that your candles will be ready.

Oils

Oils

ils are magical and multifaceted substances. Like many of the crafts in this book, oils feature prominently in the magical tradition at least in part because of their multitude of practical applications and how efficiently they are used to preserve a harvest. While raw cut plants degrade rather quickly, their properties, both magical and medicinal, can be easily infused in oil, which will carry those benefits for months or years if stored properly. For the bulk of our history, humans have lived in a world without climate control, refrigeration, or other luxuries of food preservation, making the power of preserving the harvest an essential skill. More than being a solvent for natural compounds and medicines, oil is unique in its ability to allow the absorption of these chemicals into the body, to sink into the skin and carry forth that medicine into the blood. This mechanism is at the root of the sabbatic mythos of medieval witches, who were reported to use unguents infused with poisonous psychotropics – datura, henbane, mandrake, and hemlock – to induce an astral flight to the witch's sabbath. It is also the integral mechanism of the anointing technique, in which consecrated oil suffuses into the body at cardinal points, elevating and purifying the material self. On a mundane level, this makes oil an incredibly effective route for medicinal applications, penetrating deeper into the skin than waters alone. This property of oils to store the harvest and provide medicine is enough to make them an essential household tool for the witch's cabinet, but they possess another property that makes them unrivalled as material allies for the magician. Oils burn.

Fire and the ability of a substance to burn are uniquely positioned within magic as powerful tools for working with spirits. Sublimation through fire, whether burning incenses or sacrifices, has been an important route of transmission from the human world to the spirit world since the first human cities, as this process turns matter into immaterial smoke, causing the formed to become formless. Oils do this with surprising efficiency, allowing ancient magicians to not only stoke their spiritual fires, but to capture the power of fire and wield it safely within their homes. In Agrippa's 1531 title *Three Books of Occult Philosophy*, he speaks of fire as being a "vehicle for light", and oil as being a liquor which contains the spark of light within it, in both a literal and spiritual sense. He even gives several charms for summoning ghostly images by oil, where oil is used to fix the essence of a substance such that it can be summoned again by a magician. For example, he accounts how one might infuse an oil with the skin of snakes, which, when burned, will cause serpents to appear. This property of oil, as a substance containing the generative seed of fire, was likened to its ability to house spirits, and thus made oil an important materia for offering to gods and consecrating magical tools. In Ancient Egypt, statues were enlivened and ensouled by use of scented oils, drawn across the forehead and down between the eyes.

In alchemical magic, oil is also viewed as a substance with special occult properties. In particular, the essential oils of materia, isolated by steam distillation or other extractions, are called the alchemical "sulfur", which is said to contain the "soul" of a substance. For Greek alchemists in the ancient world, the alchemical soul was equated to the psyche, the bridge which connects body and mind. This is largely due to the volatile nature of these oils, which are able to evaporate into the air and suffuse into everything, transcending the boundary between material and immaterial being, much the way that fire does. Paracelsus, often viewed as the father of Western alchemy, coined the term "essential oil" in reference to his belief that these compounds contain the quintessence of a thing – a plant, an animal, a metal – in the most purified sense. In ceremonial magic, distilling this "soul" is especially important, as the material physicality of plants and animals is viewed as a crude, impure aspect, while distillations that isolate the essential oil "soul" are viewed as having been purified of their earthly nature. It is interesting to note that these essential oils also contain the primary fragrance compounds of plants, which, as we mentioned in the Incense chapter, aligns them with the ancient tradition of magical scentcraft. Many of the magical oils listed in ancient grimoires are noted for their fragrance, and are infused with aromatic plants such as rose, galbanum, lily, spikenard, and even unpleasant aromatics like radishes. Oils would have been the primary method of perfume-making in the deeply ancient world, as these solvents capture the essential oil fragrances of plants in a way that is stronger and more shelf-stable than water, allowing them to be stored and reapproached again and again.

As a final point about the power and potency of oils, it's worth mentioning that the uniquely reflective surface offered by oils, with higher viscosity than waters and alcohols, was also viewed as a magical property. Using just a drop of consecrated

oil, a magician could turn any surface into a reflective mirror, and this is precisely the technology behind many oil-scrying rites of the ancient world. In the *Greek Magical Papyri*, several oil divination rituals are mentioned, most particularly the "princes of the thumb", which requires oil to be used both as an anointing substance to consecrate a young boy, and as the divining medium, in which the oil is spread across the boy's thumbnail, and he is encouraged to scry upon the reflective images he sees as sacred names are whispered into his ear. Lecanomancy, or divination by reading oil shapes in water, finds its origins in ancient Babylon, where numerous tablets detail specific definitions for omens read in reflective oil. Even these

rituals viewed oil as being susceptible to spirit inhabitation, as several secondary rites are given for removing witches and demons from one's scrying bowl, by virtue of the oil's perceived ability to carry spirits within it.

These various properties of oil – to preserve, to burn, to house spiritual fire, to carry fragrance, and to reflect light – are what make this special substance the magical powerhouse we know and love today. While many oil blends and creations are widely available for purchase, crafting them ourselves with deep intention will allow us to create special ritual tools catered to the needs of our individual practices. As you make your way through the recipes ahead, take note of which of these properties are invoked within each recipe, or how they can be used in your own practice to accomplish each of these various ends.

Oilmaking tools

While there are a number of different ways to craft infused oils at home, there are some essential tools that you will need for any method. These items will likely be present in your own kitchen already, but like all the crafts in this book, it's important to use tools and equipment that is not also used for cooking, to limit cross-contamination of inedible herbal ingredients. For oil crafting, you will need:

* **AIRTIGHT JARS & STORAGE VESSELS** – Oils are not indefinitely shelf-stable and will go rancid over time. Proper storage can help us extend the shelf life of our creations, and limiting the exposure of our oils to the air goes a long way. Airtight jars also prevent spills and leakage, which is very common with liquid products like oils. These vessels should be made of non-reactive glass and metal, such as Mason jars.

* **STRAINERS** – Once our oil is infused, we will need to remove our organic material. By using sieves/fine-mesh strainers and coffee filters, we can achieve a pure, filtered end product, which will go a long way in extending the shelf life of the oil.

* **POTS & STIRRERS** – For hot-method infusions, discussed below, you will need to create a simple bain-marie/double boiler. Since these pots will not come in direct contact with botanical ingredients, it is not necessary to purchase new ones specifically for this craft. Disposable wooden stirrers like bamboo skewers and chopsticks are also handy to have for stirring oils during infusion.

* **MEASURING TOOLS** – To further preserve our infusions, we will need to carefully measure preservatives, essential oils, and extracts. Droppers and measuring cups will greatly assist here, as being precise in our recipes allows us to reproduce the same creations time and time again.

Once all tools, herbs, and ingredients have been gathered, you're ready to begin infusing your own oils. The recipes ahead will outline a number of specific applications for these techniques, and give you useful starting points for developing your own unique recipes for oils and salves. While these recipes will provide detailed instructions on specific techniques, you can find a general overview of some common infusion methods below, as well as tips for making your crafting process simpler and more efficient.

Please read these instructions carefully before proceeding.

How to make oils

In this chapter, we will explore oils infused by two methods: using ultraviolet (UV) radiation and the maceration method. The UV method uses the warmth and light of the sun to gently coax our plants to surrender their natural compounds and essential oils, requiring a long, slow steep in direct beams of the sun. The maceration method relies upon using the bain-marie, a gentle heating method developed in Ancient Alexandria by Maria the Prophetess, a famous female alchemist. This process ensures that our oils never exceed the boiling temperature of water (100°C/220°F), protecting the compounds and fragrances of the plants from mutating in excess heat, which would essentially fry our plant materia in the oil.

In addition, it's important to note that these extractions require us to limit the exposure of water to our oil. Water will allow bacteria to fester, introducing microbes and other pollutants into our oil, which will speed its degradation. To limit the water you introduce to your oil, consider using dry plants for your infusions, or allowing any fresh plant materia to wilt at room temperature for

2–3 days before infusing, so that much of the plant's water content evaporates. Following this suggestion will increase your oil's shelf life and create a finer finished product.

The UV method

To infuse your oils using the light of the sun, you will need only an infusion vessel, a sunny windowsill, and time. This method is preferred by those who are in no rush and prefer a gentle infusion that uses less heat. Heat can destroy botanical fragrance, leaving delicate florals smelling "cooked" and soupy instead of aromatic and sweet. At the same time, ultraviolet radiation can slightly degrade the medicinal benefits of our oils. However, some herbalists believe that a short period of UV exposure during the infusion, followed by proper storage of the oil away from light and heat, is brief enough to protect most of these delicate compounds. While UV methods will produce more complete fragrance profiles, especially for delicate scents, needing to wait weeks, even months, for a finished product is a very obvious downside.

STEP 1 –
Pretreat the herbs

To begin a UV infusion, start with an airtight jar large enough to hold all your plant material and oil. Place your herbs in the jar, then mix in a small amount (a few tablespoons) of high-proof grain alcohol or isopropyl alcohol. This helps to liberate the active compounds of your plants, making it easier for them to infuse into the oil.

This step is not strictly necessary, but will greatly increase the potency of your infusion. Unflavoured vodkas and grain spirits are my personal preference, but keep in mind that lower-proof alcohols (60 per cent or below) will not be suitable for this project, as they contain too much water. Allow the herbs and alcohol to stand, uncovered, for 1 hour.

STEP 2 –
Add the carrier oil

When the pretreatment phase has elapsed, stir in your carrier oil, ensuring all herbs are fully liberated into the oil, and none have clumped together at the bottom. Recipes will be given within this chapter, but as a general rule, a ratio of 1:2 or 2:3 parts herbs to oil is a good place to start. Oils will have different densities and characteristics, with some being much richer and more unctuous than others. A few common choices are:

* **GRAPESEED OIL** – A very light and fast-absorbing oil, available in most grocery stores.

* **OLIVE OIL** – A richly hydrating oil with a mild fragrance of its own.

* **COCONUT OIL** – An accessible, affordable option that is deeply nourishing for the skin. While virgin coconut oils will retain the characteristic aroma, refined coconut oils will be fragrance-free.

* **ALMOND OIL** – Light upon the skin and nourishing, but unsuitable for those with nut allergies.

* **SUNFLOWER OIL** – An affordable, light oil that is known for its gentleness on sensitive skin.

* **JOJOBA OIL** – This liquid is technically a wax, but works functionally as an oil and penetrates the skin deeply.

STEP 3 –
Infuse the oil

Seal this jar and shake it well, then set it on a windowsill that receives good, strong sun for a few hours every day. This infusion can take anywhere from two weeks to a month to complete, depending upon your desired strength. Since this book is primarily concerned with magical applications over medicinal ones, the strength and concentration of our finished product is less important.

STEP 4 –
Strain the oil

When you are satisfied with the finished product, strain your oil well using a sieve/fine-mesh strainer, coffee filter, or cheesecloth into a glass bottle.

STEP 5 –
Preserve and store the oil

No matter what method you choose for your infusion, it's important to remember your preservatives. While oil can stand for a long time at room temperature, it is not 100 per cent shelf-stable, and will begin to go rancid on its own after a few months, especially if exposed to sun or heat. To combat this natural degradation, include a preservative of your choice to increase the oil's shelf life. Many essential oils, especially rosemary, thyme, and oregano, are antimicrobial and antibacterial enough to act as a preservative in sufficient quantities, though these bring their own fragrances to the oil as well. Vitamin E, a natural antioxidant, performs this function beautifully, and should be added to oils at 1–3 per cent by volume for its preserving

effects. This compound is scentless and colourless, making it the most discreet natural preservative I can name. Lab-made natural preservatives, such as benzyl alcohol or salicylic acid, are also fine choices, but require strict adherence to concentration limits in order to be safe and effective. Any of these methods will be useful in preserving your oil, but even with a preservative, oils should only be used for a maximum of 1–2 years before fresh batches are required. You will be able to spot a degeneration of your oil if it thickens or becomes waxy, loses clarity, or develops a mineral-oil-like chemical smell. These are all indications that your oil is past its prime and needs to be replaced. Oils should be stored in airtight vessels, away from direct sunlight and temperature fluctuations, and used within two years. If your oil is older than one year, check for signs of rancidity before use, to ensure that your preservatives have stood the test of time.

The maceration method

The benefits of the maceration method are obvious. Compared to the UV method, maceration takes a fraction of the time (1–2 hours) to complete, but it does require special equipment. This method also uses direct exposure to heat, which may alter the fragrance profile of your finished oil in undesirable ways. However, if your finished product will have essential oils or other fragrances added, perhaps this is not so important. Maceration extraction can still pull out lovely plant perfumes, especially from dry spices, but experimentation will be required to achieve the desired effect from fresh plants or flowers. If you're looking to create an oil in just a few hours as opposed to a few weeks, this preparation method will be right for you.

STEP 1 –
Pretreat the herbs

I recommend pretreating your herbs with alcohol just as with the UV method (see pages 171–4), as this produces a better extraction no matter which method you choose.

STEP 2 –
Add the carrier oil

Following the directions from the UV method (see pages 171–4), select a carrier oil appropriate for your project, measure out the desired amount, and stir the herbs into the oil. Pour this mixture into a heatproof glass jar or metal heating vessel.

STEP 3 –
Infuse the oil

Maceration requires us to set up a bain-marie/double boiler, to ensure the oil stays at an even temperature. To do this at home easily, place your heatproof glass jar or heating vessel into a large stock pot, then fill the pot with water around your oil vessel. As the water heats, the oil within the jar will heat as well, but will keep heating temperatures consistent and gentle. It's important to fill the pot with water to the same level as your oil jar, so that the oil within heats evenly. Bring the water to a simmer and allow to gestate for at least 30 minutes to 1 hour. Allow the oil to cool completely before handling.

STEP 4 –
Strain the oil

When finished, strain your oil completely using a sieve/fine mesh strainer, coffee filter, or cheesecloth into an airtight glass bottle. Press the herbs gently to ensure all oil is expressed. Discard the herbs when finished.

STEP 5 –
Preserve and store the oil

Add your preservative (see notes on preserving in the UV method – page 174) and store away from direct sunlight and temperature fluctuations. Just as with UV oils, these should be used within two years.

Infusion procedures are chosen to play to the strengths of each of the methods within this chapter, but both will produce infused oils nonetheless. You may find, in your own experiments, that you prefer one method over the other, in which case I encourage you to use the method that you prefer, or to conduct your own experiments that reveal the differences between these two simple extraction methods.

ALL-PURPOSE ANOINTING OIL

While nothing in magic can ever be truly "all-purpose", you can sometimes find recipes so useful that they become helpful standards to have on hand. Many magical preparations designed to enhance potency of our charms or ensure magical efficacy work this way, such that almost every charm or ritual can benefit from their addition. This is the spirit in which this recipe was written, based on an anointing oil I have tinkered with for the better part of a decade.

This recipe uses an ingredient for each of the seven planetary spheres, infused in olive oil, which is the traditional holy oil of many ancient magical traditions. Bay leaves bring in the prophetic powers of the Sun, elder the cunning influences of the Moon, hazel leaves for the magic of Mercury, perfumed lemon balm for Venus, aromatic pine for Mars, delightful fresh nutmeg for Jupiter, and mushroom stands in for chthonic Saturn. Infused for one full lunation, this oil is made in the style of many traditional astrological preparations that serve an all-purpose consecrating function, invoking all seven of the classical spheres as a single beam of all-potentiality. To prepare this oil, gather your ingredients on the eve of the full moon.

Makes: 250ml/9fl oz/1 cup oil
Prep time: 1 hour, plus 1 month infusing

FOR THE OIL
* 1 tablespoon crushed bay leaves
* 1 tablespoon dried elderflower
* 1 tablespoon hazel leaves
* 1 tablespoon lemon balm
* 1 teaspoon dried pine resin
* 1 teaspoon scraped nutmeg
* 1 tablespoon finely grated dried mushrooms (any type) or mushroom powder
* Airtight jar
* 3 tablespoons high-proof grain alcohol or isopropyl alcohol
* 250ml/9fl oz/1 cup extra virgin olive oil
* Glass storage bottle
* Preservatives/essential oils (see page 172)

1 If pretreating your herbs, mix all your plant material in an airtight jar, then add the alcohol, allowing the herbs and alcohol to stand, uncovered, for 1 hour.

2 Stir in the carrier oil.

3 Before sealing the jar, speak into the opening to the plant spirits contained in this spell. Remind them of their divine nature, and request that they lend the blessings of their ruling planets each time they are called upon. Ask that they enliven this oil and make it a potent vehicle for drawing the powers of the seven spheres into your work. If you want to go deeper, you may even read invocations to the seven planets, or draw their symbols upon your infusion jar. You could craft a unique sigil just for this charm, which symbolizes your own potency and power as a magician.

4 Seal the jar and allow it to infuse on a sunny windowsill for 1 month until the next full moon rises.

5 When the month is complete, strain your oil into a glass bottle. Stir in any preservatives or essential oils you wish to use.

6 Use this oil to dot the temples, heart, and hands before magical operations, or to anoint magical objects after they are cleansed.

LUNAR ANOINTING OIL

In magical traditions throughout the world, it is the mysterious Moon who appears again and again as the ruler of enchantment. She is the goddess and teacher of witches, the ally of ceremonial magicians, the illuminatrix of astrologers, and the evening lamp of poets. As earth-bound beings, the moon is our closest heavenly body, whose presence and predictable cycles puts us deeply in touch with primordial reality and the vastness of the universe. The moon is an unparalleled ally in magic and manifestation, as evidenced by her central position in magical traditions from the first human societies to today.

This recipe for a lunar anointing oil uses nine ingredients (nine being one of the numbers of the moon in Western planetary magic) of a lunar nature, and is crafted over the course of a full lunation, from one full moon to the next. The oil will not be especially aromatic, as herbs of a lunar nature are known for producing a more gentle, light perfume, although you will certainly smell the delicious star anise, herbaceous mugwort, and violet-like orris root. It is best to use fractionated coconut oil here, as this slow UV infusion will require the oil to stay liquid at room temperature.

To prepare this oil, gather your ingredients on the eve of the full moon.

Makes: 250ml/9fl oz/1 cup oil
Prep time: 1 hour, plus 1 month infusing

FOR THE OIL
* 1 tablespoon dried mugwort
* 1 teaspoon orris root
* 1 teaspoon poppy seeds
* 1 teaspoon marshmallow root
* 1 teaspoon dried yarrow
* 1 teaspoon hops
* 1 star anise
* Dried petals from 1 white rose
* Airtight jar
* 3 tablespoons high-proof grain alcohol or isopropyl alcohol (optional)
* 250ml/9fl oz/1 cup coconut oil
* Glass storage bottle
* Preservatives/essential oils (see page 172)

1 If pretreating your herbs beforehand, mix all your plant material in an airtight jar, then add the alcohol, allowing the herbs and alcohol to stand, uncovered, for 1 hour.

2 Stir in the coconut oil, then seal the jar and allow to infuse on a windowsill where the jar can receive both sunlight and moonlight until the next full moon rises.

3 On the next full moon, strain your oil into a glass storage bottle. Stir in any preservatives or essential oils you wish to use.

4 You can mark this bottle in lunar sigils using silver ink and consecrate it during your next full moon ritual with the smoke of frankincense and hymns to lunar divinities or to the Moon herself. Consider adding a small piece of moonstone to the bottle, and use to anoint yourself, your pendulums or scrying stones, and any important altarwares used specifically in moon rituals. For all works of lunar magic, from full moon rites to lunar arts like divination and dreamwork, this simple anointing oil is a welcome addition.

WARDING OIL

Apotropaic magic, used to ward off evil and misfortune, is one of the most ancient forms of witchcraft. These passive charms are designed to avert disaster before it begins, offering protection by virtue of turning away all negativity and ill-influence. Medieval gargoyles, horseshoe talismans, and Ancient Greek engravings of the Gorgoneion are all examples of apotropaia, using a fearful or powerful image to turn back other, more loathsome foes. In modern vernacular, witches use warding magic to achieve the same effect. This recipe provides a simple consecrated warding oil, to be used by itself in apotropaic magic, or as part of larger workings to stop evil in its tracks. Using potent herbs of protection, specifically those under the rulership of the malefic planets Mars and Saturn, this oil is particularly suited for magic involving deep cleansing, fierce protection, and the setting of immovable boundaries.

Makes: 250ml/9fl oz/1 cup oil
Prep time: 1 hour, plus cooling

FOR THE OIL

* 2 tablespoons dried wormwood
* 2 tablespoons dried St John's wort
* 2 tablespoons dried rue
* Small handful of dried cedar fronds
* Heatproof airtight jar
* Stock pot
* 3 tablespoons high-proof grain alcohol or isopropyl alcohol (optional)
* 250ml/9fl oz/1 cup grapeseed oil
* Sieve/fine-mesh strainer, coffee filter, or cheesecloth
* Glass storage bottle

1 If pretreating your herbs, mix all your plant material in a jar (reserving ½ a teaspoon of the mixture for the consecration ritual if desired), then add the alcohol, allowing the herbs and alcohol to stand, uncovered, for a few hours or overnight.

2 Add the oil to the jar, then create a bain-marie by placing the jar in a stock pot and filling the pot with water to the same level as the oil in the jar. Bring the water to a gentle simmer over a low heat. If you haven't pretreated your herbs, mix them together in a small bowl, then add to the jar. Allow to infuse for 1 hour. If you chose to pretreat your herbs, they should be especially fragrant.

3 When the hour has passed, take the pot off the heat and allow the jar to cool until it can be safely handled, then strain the oil into a glass storage bottle. Stir in any preservatives or essential oils you wish to use.

4 To consecrate this oil for use in drawing boundaries, protection magic, and marking the edges of a safe space, consecrate it on a Tuesday during the hour of Saturn. Burn Martial plants, such as the ones contained within this recipe, and pass the bottle of oil through the smoke. Recite orations to Mars, the planet that governs boundaries and defensive magic, and draw a sigil of protection in red ink upon the bottle. Use this oil to ward your home by dotting the corners of your door frames, drawing sigils upon your windows, and lining your thresholds. You may also use it to consecrate protection amulets, or use in personal protection charms, such as anointing the hands and feet before travel.

DIVINATION OIL

The desire to tap into greater powers of perception is as old as magic itself. While some of us may possess our own innate sense of intuition and cunning, there is a deep tradition of crafting potions and preparations to enhance one's psychic abilities. In Ancient Greek and Roman magic, great care was taken to consecrate oils in elaborate rituals that could grant visions and prophecy when applied to the eyelids. In medieval Europe, flower charms crafted on St John's Eve could give dream-visions of future loves if tucked beneath the pillow before bed. In the early 20th century, with the rise of spiritualism and esotericism, mass-market perfumes and incenses began to be marketed as magical ingredients, capable of enhancing natural or latent psychic powers.

Using herbs in this way, for their ability to help us to see deeper and further than we can on our own, has been a tool employed by witches and magicians throughout human history. The six ingredients in this recipe are among the most potent of enchanters' herbs, all specifically associated with enhancing magical potency, sharpening our focus, and granting diviners greater powers of second sigh. The resulting oil is resinous, aromatic, and toasty, with a stimulating fragrance of nuts and herbs and the sweet perfume of opopanax, also called "sweet myrrh". Adding additional fragrances or essential oils to our blend is never required for magical preparations, but for this naturally aromatic oil, its own complex perfume is delightful by itself

---

Makes: 250ml/9fl oz/1 cup oil

Prep time: 1 hour, plus cooling

FOR THE OIL

* 9 bay leaves
* 1 tablespoon dried yarrow
* 1 tablespoon dried clary sage
* 1 tablespoon dried vervain
* 1 teaspoon ground opopanax resin
* Heatproof airtight jar
* 3 tablespoons high-proof grain alcohol or isopropyl alcohol (optional)
* 250ml/9fl oz/1 cup hazelnut oil
* Stock pot
* Sieve/fine-mesh strainer, coffee filter, or cheesecloth
* Glass storage bottle
* Preservatives/essential oils (see page 172)

I If pretreating your herbs, mix all your plant material in a jar, then add the alcohol, allowing the herbs and alcohol to stand, uncovered, for a few hours or overnight.

2 Add the oil to the jar, then create a bain-marie by placing the jar in a stock pot and filling the pot with water to the same level as the oil in the jar. Bring the water to a gentle simmer over a low heat. If you haven't pretreated your herbs, mix them together in a small bowl, then add to the jar. Allow the oil to infuse for 1 hour. If you chose to pretreat your herbs, they should be especially fragrant.

3 When the hour has passed, take the pot off the heat and allow the jar to cool until it can be safely handled, then strain the oil into a glass storage bottle. Stir in any preservatives or essential oils you wish to use.

4 You may also add crystals associated with divination, such as moonstone or amethyst. You may even craft a sigil to enhance your second sight, draw this on a bay leaf, and slip it into the oil bottle for an extra boost. Use this preparation to dot the hands and temples before Tarot readings, dreamwork, or any of your other vision-seeking works of magic.

FLYING OINTMENT

Flying Ointment is a preparation that defines medieval European witchcraft. These preparations were documented extensively by witch hunters, and were reported to contain foul ingredients such as the rendered fat of unbaptized babes and poisonous, psychotropic plants. These hell-broths were believed to be the vehicle that transported witches to their astral sabbaths with the Devil, enabling them to "fly" either literally or psychically. While limited evidence exists for the use of psychotropic flying ointments among actual practitioners, this iconic preparation has shaped the image of the witch significantly enough to become a part of her iconography. In the modern world, practitioners tap into this lineage by brewing salves of vision-giving plants, like mugwort and wormwood of the Artemisia family, or hypnotic sedatives like blue lotus and damiana. These transdermal salves are much gentler than traditional flying ointments, retaining the same name only as an homage to the iconic history and folklore that inspired them.

Makes: 250ml/9fl oz/1 cup oil
Prep time: 1 hour 30 minutes, plus cooling

FOR THE OIL
* 6 tablespoons mugwort
* 4 tablespoons damiana
* 3 tablespoons wormwood
* 3 whole blue lotus flowers
* 2 heatproof airtight jars
* 3 tablespoons high-proof grain alcohol or isopropyl alcohol (optional)
* 250ml/9fl oz/1 cup hempseed oil
* Stock pot
* 3½ tablespoons beeswax pastilles
* Preservatives/essential oils (see page 172)
* 225ml/8fl oz storage jar

1 If pretreating your herbs, mix all your plant material in a jar, then add the alcohol, allowing the herbs and alcohol to stand, uncovered, for 1 hour.

2 Add the oil to the jar, then create a bain-marie by placing the jar in a stock pot and filling the pot with water to the same level as the oil in the jar. Bring the water to a gentle simmer over a low heat. If you haven't pretreated your herbs, you may simply mix them together in a small bowl, then add to the jar with the oil. Allow the oil to infuse for 1 hour. If you chose to pretreat your herbs, they should be especially fragrant.

3 When the hour has passed, take the pot off the heat and allow the jar to cool until it can be safely handled. Strain the preparation into another jar, pressing your botanicals to ensure all the oil is expressed.

4 Place the jar in your stock pot, then bring the water to a gentle simmer once more. When the oil begins to warm, stir in the beeswax until completely melted, then immediately remove from the heat.

5 When the oil is still liquid but cool enough to touch with your fingertips, stir in any preservatives or essential oils you wish to use.

6 Pour the finished salve into a 225ml/8fl oz storage jar, then allow it to cool until fully set.

7 While this salve won't induce an altered state like medieval flying ointments, it can be used before engaging in trance and vision work. It is especially effective when applied before bed to encourage potent dreams and visions in sleep. To use this salve, work a lentil-sized amount of ointment into the skin on temples and pulse points, like the inside of the wrist, as well as the soles of the feet and across the eyelids.

OIL OF ABRAMELIN

This enigmatic historical recipe has seen many iterations over the centuries, with varying lists of ingredients and preparation methods. This recipe originates in the famous medieval grimoire *The Book of Abramelin*, but bears a great similarity to the ancient biblical recipe for holy oil found in the book of Exodus. In this medieval recipe, the magician is instructed to prepare an anointing oil by infusing olive oil with myrrh resin, calamus root, and two related spices, cinnamon and cassia. This process is carried out "as is done by chemists" – meaning the oil is infused over a low heat until the essential oils are extracted from the plants, then distilled. This emphasis on distillation of the plants has led to more modern editions of this recipe, like the one published by Aleister Crowley and the OTO (Ordo Templi Orientis, a magical order based on Crowley's teachings which formed in the early 20th century), to favour using proportions of essential oils (a distilled extract) over the whole plants themselves. These versions of Oil of Abramelin are certainly easier to prepare, but the finished result differs extremely from the original recipe, even if the ingredients do technically fit the bill.

While the method presented in this recipe is simplified from the original medieval version, it preserves the initial step of macerating the plants with the oil. You may choose to add additional essential oils of your own, but these will only add to the fragrance of your oil, not its magical potency per se. As cinnamon essential oils can be irritating to the skin in high concentrations, this recipe follows traditional proportions to produce a gentler infusion.

Makes: 120ml/4fl oz/½ cup oil
Prep time: 2 hours, plus cooling

FOR THE OIL

* 2 tablespoons powdered myrrh resin
* 2 tablespoons cassia chips
* 2 tablespoons calamus root
* 1 tablespoon cinnamon chips
* Heatproof airtight jar
* 3 tablespoons high-proof grain alcohol or isopropyl alcohol (optional)
* 120ml/4fl oz/½ cup extra virgin olive oil
* Stock pot
* Sieve/fine-mesh strainer, coffee filter or cheesecloth
* Glass storage bottle
* Preservatives/essential oils (see page 172)

1 If pretreating your herbs, mix all your plant material in a jar, then add the alcohol, allowing the herbs and alcohol to stand, uncovered, for 1 hour.

2 Add the oil to the jar, then create a bain-marie by placing the jar in a pot and filling the pot with water to the same level as the oil in the jar. Bring the water to a gentle simmer over a low heat. If you haven't pretreated your herbs, you may simply mix them together in a small bowl, then add to the jar with the oil. Allow the oil to infuse for 1 hour.

3 When the hour has passed, take the pot off the heat and allow the jar to cool until it can be safely handled, then strain the oil into a glass storage bottle. Stir in any preservatives or essential oils you wish to use.

4 The original recipe in *The Book of Abramelin* instructs that this oil be stored beneath the practitioner's altar, and that it be used in accordance with the book's proposed system of magic. However, this oil has found its way into many traditions since, with broad use in Thelema and ceremonial magic, Jewish kabbalah, and even as a single ingredient outside of these formalized systems of magic. Use in works of consecration, purifying magic, and in seeking one's Holy Guardian Angel.

SATURN OIL

When I first began my work with planetary magic, I was not a friend of Saturn. The greater malefic seemed too heavy and arduous to be useful, ruling over responsibility, death, taxes, and the least fun aspects of existence. As a triple-Gemini, my mutability and experimental approaches felt little in common with Saturn's timeless traditionality, opposing my desire for freedom with its emphasis on boundaries and limits. But Father Time, one of the mythopoetic avatars of Saturn, is quite patient, and as I matured into adulthood, the deep wisdom of the seventh sphere became fully apparent.

Saturn is the planet of rot and rebirth, promising that suffering and healing are two necessary aspects of being alive. While Saturn is most known as the sphere of curses and poisons, the goth kid of planetary magic, it also governs the fiercest forms of protection magic, and a slow but certain delivery of return for investment. Saturn and Mars are both planets that are said to rule boundaries and limitations, but they do so in very different ways. While Mars may rule physical boundaries, such as the wall between one room and another, Saturn governs immovable limits that form the boundaries of what is possible, such as the limit between life and death. As a planetary ally, Saturn's immovability and constancy present certain frustrations, but there is also an unmatched dependability within this sphere, making it incredibly useful for magicians who work to bring the subtle world into reality.

Makes: 250ml/9fl oz/1 cup oil
Prep time: 2 hours, plus cooling

FOR THE OIL

* 2 tablespoons blackberry leaf
* 2 tablespoons horsetail fern
* 2 English ivy leaves
* 1 teaspoon cumin seeds
* 1 teaspoon ground myrrh resin
* Heatproof airtight jar
* Stock pot
* 3 tablespoons high-proof grain alcohol or isopropyl alcohol (optional)
* 250ml/9fl oz/1 cup hempseed oil
* Sieve/fine-mesh strainer, coffee filter, or cheesecloth
* Glass storage bottle
* Preservatives/essential oils (see page 172)

1 To prepare this oil, gather your ingredients on a Saturday at a Saturnian hour.

2 If pretreating your herbs, mix all your plant material in a jar, then add the alcohol, allowing the herbs and alcohol to stand, uncovered, for 1 hour.

3 Add the oil to the jar, then create a bain-marie by placing the jar in a stock pot and filling the pot with water to the same level as the oil in the jar. Bring the water to a gentle simmer over a low heat. If you haven't pretreated your herbs, mix them together in a small bowl, then add to the jar. Allow the oil to infuse for 1 hour. This oil will smell resinous and green, and if the herbs have been awakened with alcohol before infusing, the oil will become very rich and dark. These earthy aromas and dark colours are very Saturnine and will be an indication that your infusion is getting stronger.

4 When the hour has passed, take the pot off the heat and allow the jar to cool until it can be safely handled, then strain the oil into a glass storage bottle. Stir in any preservatives or essential oils you wish to use.

5 Adorn the bottle with the symbol of Saturn and use as an ingredient in all forms of Saturnine magic, such as necromancy, funeral magic, cursework and malefica, apotropaic magic, or rites to draw powerful boundaries.

OLEORESINS

Botanical resins are unique ingredients and they have a special place within the witch's workshop. Made of both hydrophilic gum and hydrophobic resin, these crystalized plant saps are often very fragrant, owing to a high density of fragrance oils and medicinal compounds. When these substances are extracted through an oil infusion, the resulting serum is called an oleoresin. After infusing over a gentle heat, the hydrophilic gum and residue is filtered off and discarded, leaving behind a potent serum into which the hydrophobic resin has fully melted. This oleoextraction is the best way to capture the medicinal and fragrant properties of plant resins, which contain high amounts of essential oils and antioxidants. For example, frankincense oleoresins contain boswellic acids, which are powerful anti-aging

compounds used in skincare. Benzoin oleoresin is also used in skincare, owing to its anti-inflammatory and skin-clearing properties. Pine oleoresins are used aromatherapeutically to open the airways and relieve stress or muscle tension. These perfumed extractions can be used on their own, with essential oils added to enhance the natural fragrance, or set into a long-lasting salve with a little beeswax.

To prepare an oleoresin, choose your ingredients carefully. The neutral carrier oil should have little fragrance of its own, and be able to withstand a little heat from a slow, gentle infusion. Grapeseed oil is a strong candidate, as it is inexpensive, easily found in grocery stores, and quickly sinks into the skin. Your resins should be of good quality and powdered as finely as possible to ensure the best infusion.

Makes: 250ml/9fl oz/1 cup oil
Prep time: 1 hour, plus cooling and straining

FOR THE OIL
* 250ml/9fl oz/1 cup neutral carrier oil
* Heatproof airtight jar
* Stock pot
* 115g/4oz powdered resin, such as frankincense, benzoin, myrrh, opopanax, labdanum, pine, cedar, etc.
* Oven mitts or heatproof gloves
* Sieve/fine-mesh strainer, coffee filter, or cheesecloth
* Glass storage bottle

1 Pour the oil into a glass jar, then create a bain-marie by placing the jar in a stock pot and filling the pot with water to the same level as the oil in the jar. Bring the water to a gentle simmer over a low heat. Stir in your powdered resin, then allow the oil to infuse for 1 hour, stirring frequently. This process will be very aromatic, and it is important to keep the heat at a low simmer so as not to distort the fragrance.

2 When the hour has passed, take the pot off the heat. Use oven mitts or heatproof gloves to carefully remove the hot jar from the water, then strain the oil while hot into a glass storage bottle. The oil will become more viscous as it cools, so it will be easier to strain while still warm. Stir in any preservatives or essential oils you wish to use.

3 Beyond using these oils in skincare for their medicinal benefits, these aromatic resins are highly prized offerings and materia magica, especially by way of their fragrance. In situations where incense cannot be burned, such as around children or within closed spaces, these oils carry the full energetic imprint of these sacred plant allies, fragrance and all.

TAPPUTI'S ROYAL SALVE

In reading the few recipes left behind by Tapputi, the world's first recorded perfumer, there is a great mystery that emerges. The distillation techniques she describes are advanced, but use tools and vessels that are unknown to the modern world. Many of the ingredients she cites, fresh flowers and aromatic grasses, are either extinct or untranslatable, adding a frustrating impermeability to her recipes. Many historians would give anything to know what her perfumes and ointments truly smelled like, but the fragments of her work that remain, broken and half-translated, can only paint a partial picture. Inspired by a surviving fragment of her recipe for a royal perfume, this salve uses many of the herbs and fragrances mentioned in her ancient writings, infused using simplified techniques and procedures. As most of us will not have Tapputi's elaborate distillation equipment at home, essential oils will play an important role in the fragrance of this salve. However, just like the original recipe, this herbal oil is slowly infused in conjunction with the moon and stars, building a lasting fragrance through multiple phases of infusion. As such, you should infuse the oil on a full moon that occurs in a Venusian sign, like Taurus or Libra.

Makes: 250ml/9fl oz/1 cup oil
Prep time: 2 hours, plus 1 month infusing

FOR THE OIL
* 1 tablespoon calamus root
* 2 tablespoons powdered myrrh
* 3 tablespoons dried rose petals
* 2.5cm/1in piece of fresh lemongrass
* Heatproof airtight jars
* 3 tablespoons high-proof grain alcohol or isopropyl alcohol (optional)
* 250ml/9fl oz/1 cup extra virgin olive oil
* Stock pot
* 3½ tablespoons beeswax pastilles
* 20 drops rose essential oil
* 20 drops nagarmotha essential oil
* 20 drops balsam fir essential oil
* Preservatives (see page 172)
* 225ml/8fl oz storage jar

1 While this step is optional, I highly recommend pretreating these herbs with alcohol before infusing, as this will carry so much more of the fragrance of these plants into your final preparation. Additionally, the fresh lemongrass should be pounded with the back of a knife to break its fibres and release the essential oils. As Tapputi's recipes were known for their powerful perfume, these steps feel important to emphasize. Mix all your plant material in a jar, then add the alcohol, allowing the herbs and alcohol to stand, uncovered, for 1 hour.

2 Stir in the oil, then seal the jar. Allow the herbs to infuse on a sunny windowsill for one full lunar cycle.

3 Strain the oil into a clean jar, then create a bain-marie by placing the jar in a stock pot and filling the pot with water to the same level as the oil in the jar. Bring the water to a gentle simmer over a low heat. When the oil begins to warm, stir in the beeswax until completely melted, then immediately remove from the heat.

4 When the oil is still liquid but is cool enough to touch with your fingertips, stir in the essential oils and any preservatives you wish to use.

5 Pour the finished salve into a 225ml/8fl oz storage jar, and allow it to cool until fully set.

6 While there are no recorded magical uses for this recipe, this salve can be used as a nourishing all-over body moisturizer, or consecrated under Venus to be a helpful ingredient in glamour and love magic.

ROSE OIL

What is it about the rose that captivates humans so completely? This iconic flower has existed as a symbol of love, desire, and unrivalled beauty since the ancient world, and has held a privileged position in magic for these reasons. In Ancient Egypt, the rose was one of the sacred flowers, under the rulership of Isis herself. A multitude of charms in the Greek Magical Papyri call on rose oil specifically, citing its use as a common magical ingredient to conjure spirits and to induce love. In the 16th century, the Catholic Church sanctioned the use of beads made entirely from rose petals for the creation of rosaries, though these rose-beads had been in use since at least the time of the Crusades. Even Hildegard Von Bingen, an 11th-century Christian mystic and abbess, believed that every healing medicine could be helped by adding a bit of rose.

In planetary herbalism, the rose is ruled by Venus, the sphere of harmony, pleasure, community, and delight. Venus is the source of creative inspiration and engenders friendship and intimacy between those who are under her influence. It is for this reason that rose is favoured not only for love charms, but also in spells which involve relationships of any kind, such as enlisting the aid of spirits or magical helpers. However, the peace-loving sphere of Venus is also known to be a fierce protectress, especially over lovers, families, and the innocent. Where these sumptuous, benevolent Venusian influences can be helpful, this rose oil will be a useful ally, bringing in influences from three aspects of the rose: its perfumed petals, its plump and nutritious fruits, and its protective thorns.

Makes: 250ml/9fl oz/1 cup oil
Prep time: 1 hour, plus cooling

FOR THE OIL
* 30g (about ¾ cup) dried rose petals
* 3 tablespoons dried rosehips
* 6 rose thorns
* 100 drops rose essential oil
* Heatproof airtight jar
* 3 tablespoons high-proof grain alcohol or isopropyl alcohol (optional)
* 250ml/9fl oz/1 cup rosehip oil
* Stock pot
* Sieve/fine-mesh strainer, coffee filter, or cheesecloth
* Glass storage bottle
* Preservatives/essential oils (see page 172)

1 To prepare this oil, gather your ingredients on a Friday at a Venusian hour.

2 While this first step is optional, I highly recommend pretreating these herbs with alcohol before infusing, as this will carry so much more of the fragrance and colour of the rose petals into your final preparation. Mix all your plant material in a glass jar, then add the alcohol, allowing the herbs and alcohol to stand, uncovered, for a few hours or overnight.

3 Add the rosehip oil to the jar, then create a bain-marie by placing the jar in a stock pot and filling the pot with water to the same level as the oil in the jar. Bring the water to a gentle simmer over a low heat. If you haven't pretreated your herbs, simply mix them together in a small bowl, then add to oil within the jar. Allow the oil to infuse for 1 hour.

4 When the hour has passed, take the pot off the heat and allow the jar to cool until it can be safely handled, then strain the oil into a glass storage bottle. Stir in any preservatives or essential oils you wish to use.

5 Use this oil for charms of love, for drawing assistants and helpers, for honouring spirits, and for sanctifying magic of all sorts.

Powders

Powders

owdered plants as magical materia have a very deep historical root, even if their use has fallen off within the modern era. We may be used to seeing some ritual and spell powders appear in Santeria and rootwork, like the famous cascarilla powder made from the pulverized eggshells of black hens, but preparations like these, where powder is the main ingredient in a spell, are few and far between. While modern witches may be more familiar with working oils, candles, crystals, and perfumes, history paints a very different picture of powder magic, and by studying these spells from ancient magicians, we can discover new applications and charms from this most humble, but extremely powerful, technique.

There are certainly some practical reasons why magicians may choose to work with powders over any other method. First, powdered plants store very well for long periods of time, allowing us to capture plants at the height of their season and preserve them for use throughout the rest of the year. Powders made from dried plants will keep indefinitely if stored under proper conditions, away from moisture, light, and heat. Especially in the case of ephemeral seasonal plants like lily of the valley or narcissus, which only bloom for a brief while, capturing these blossoms and preserving them may be the only chance a magician has for accessing these allies until their next short season returns. When we consider the importance of magical harvesting days like Midsummer and Beltane, where plants picked on these days are said to produce additional magical benefits, the emphasis on preserving our harvest becomes

doubly significant. Powders also allow a magician to homogenize an entire crop, containing the full plant – roots, stems, leaves, flowers, and barks – all within one teaspoon of perfectly blended powder. This application allows us to use all parts of a plant in a very efficient way, invoking the geni of the whole plant with a simple pinch.

Even in this dried and pulverized state, powders still retain many of the iconic qualities of the original plants, particularly their colours and fragrance. The most ancient paints made by humans are concocted from mineral and plant powders, which have survived tens of thousands of years and are, in many cases, still legible today. As we discussed in the chapter on Natural Dyes, harnessing the power of colour for magic is a practice with deeply ancient roots, and for the bulk of human history, this magic has been accessed through working with pigmented powders. Because of their stark, bold colours, powders have often been used in boundary-drawing magic, particularly in creating safe, accessible boundaries for working magical operations. In Ancient Mesopotamia and Sumeria, ground grain plants like barley and wheat were used in drawing the white lines of ritual circles, called zisurru. In Ancient Rome, blessed white flour prepared by the Vestal Virgins, called *mola salsa*, was used in both official and personal rituals to denote an object or space as sacred, and was used to mark the hearth within the home, as well as the foreheads of animals who were about to be sacrificed. In the Middle Ages, the geometric demarcation lines and sacred names inscribed in magic circles were drawn in chalk made from gypsum, which possessed a very bold white pigment, allowing magicians to use less powder for the same operations.

These powders similarly retain the fragrance of these herbs, breaking open cell walls making the volatile essential oil fragrances of these plants more available. Scent magic is also uniquely privileged within witch history, and without finer methods of extracting plant fragrance, such as distillation or infusion, the best results are obtained by simply using powdered herbs. These fragrant dusts are called upon as offerings and single-herb incenses throughout ancient magic, lending their potency by virtue of their powerful perfumes. One such charm from the *Book of Secrets of Albertus Magnus*[xii] calls for the use of colourful powdered minerals like vermillion and lapis lazuli combined with fragrant powdered pennyroyal to produce solid perfume pearls which, when inhaled, will give the magician visions of spirits and "infinite marvels".

As scentcraft is a form of magic prized for its ability to move unseen, capable of influencing a target while being invisible to the naked eye, powder magic has also become associated with working invisibly. Most of us wouldn't think twice about a few specks of dust on an outstretched hand, a love letter, or across a friend's front doorstep, and this is precisely the mechanism that makes powder magic so useful. In the Middle Ages, powders were an important route of dispersal for love magic, with many potions occurring in powder form rather than liquid form, so they could be dispersed into the food and drink of one's target with ease. In American hoodoo and rootwork, the West African tradition of foot-track magic, or sprinkling powders in a target's shoes or over their walking path, could directly affect their fate and wellbeing. Hoodoo practitioners also make use of common cosmetics, such as aromatic body powders, to work subtle glamour magics, or dust letters, job applications, and legal papers in magic powders to influence their outcome upon receipt. Additionally, because powders are ground to impossibly fine granules, they are believed to have an overpowering effect, in that they can be dispersed widely and invisibly to fill an entire space, undetected. One unique example from *The Petit Albert*,[xi] a famous French book of spells, appears in the chapter ahead, which calls for the magician to blow a magic powder across a lively party, making the celebrants rowdy enough to dance topless. This all-pervasive property of powders is a cornerstone of their unique magic, and makes them a strong choice for subtle commanding and compelling spells of all kinds.

It's interesting to think about a plant preparation that can be used for both concealing and revealing in this way, prized for its ability to stand out with bright pigments and also be employed in utter secrecy. At the same time, it's often said in witchcraft that a plant or object which is used for one thing may also issue command over its opposite, such as plants and talismans of Mars, which are used to issue curses as well as shield from malefic magic. Such is the nature of the magic powder, creating visible marks or casting subtle enchantments according to the witch's will. When you consider that many powder charms involve demarking ritual space, it could be said that these spells use powders to reveal and conceal simultaneously, creating a container for summoning spirits while enclosing the magician in a safe nucleus, protected from harm. As you move through the recipes ahead and work these charms for yourself, consider how these powders interact with this energetic dichotomy, and how these tools can be mastered to produce a wide range of visible and invisible magics, all of your own design.

Powder tools

Mixing magical powders at home is a breeze. Compared to other botanical crafts and techniques, powders require very little equipment to prepare, and no special ingredients like binders, fixatives, or solvents. Other than an emphasis on using dry plant material (as only dry plants can be powdered), there are very few technical notes to be made about the powdering process. It's very hard to go wrong! On a fundamental level, most powders you will make will be the same – a blend of pulverized herbs, roots, and resins. This simplicity is deceiving, as powders can be employed to innumerable ends to work countless spells and charms, as the variety of recipes in this chapter can attest. In making your own magical powders, you will want to ensure you have a few simple tools on hand:

* **GRINDING & PROCESSING TOOLS** – These items will be the most important for powder-making. For magic powders which are meant to be employed discreetly, a fine, even grind is ideal. Mortar and pestles can work very well here, as do other analogue methods for grinding herbs, like manual spice grinders. However, for dense roots, barks, and stems, an electric spice grinder or food processor will be preferable, and will cut your process time down significantly. Electric tools can be a great asset in powder-crafting, but be careful to avoid heating up your plant material with mechanical engines, as this can cause some plants, especially gums and resins, to soften and clog machinery. Using the pulse setting will be helpful here.

* **SIFTING TOOLS** – To ensure the proper fineness of your grains, sifting tools like sieves/fine-mesh strainers and tamises will be necessary. It is always recommended to sift your powders, to ensure that all elements are evenly ground, and to remove any clumps caused by moisture.

* **BRUSHES** – These are not the tools that immediately come to mind in making powders, but practical experience has shown no better tool for ensuring that every last bit of magic dust can be collected. Firm-bristled brushes, like those for paint or makeup, can be so helpful in cleaning out grinding equipment, sweeping powders into storage vessels, and even employing magic powders discreetly. For example, while powders

can certainly be pinched between fingers, a brush dipped into a powder jar and then tapped to release the dust within can help keep fingers clean and stray granules to a minimum.

* **RESPIRATORY PROTECTION & PPE** – Powders produce compounds so small and fine that they can be easily breathed in without noticing. This is not usually dangerous, but they can flare up asthma and allergies for folks with sensitive respiratory systems. However, the recipes in this chapter do call for certain compounds which would be dangerous to inhale, like plaster of Paris, and these recipes note the importance of wearing proper PPE while crafting. As a baseline for best practices, wearing a respiratory mask is always a good call when working with powdered herbs, and can help protect your skin, sinuses, and lungs from irritation.

* **PROPER STORAGE JARS** – Airtight storage jars are recommended for most botanical preparations within this book, but they are especially important for storing powders. Microscopic water molecules can enter jars that are not airtight, making your powders clump up, cake, and stick together, necessitating the process of grinding and sifting all over again. Additionally, for powders that should not be breathed in, like ground poisonous plants, plasters, or fine salts, airtight jars help contain the risk of contamination. For storing these kinds of compounds, take care to open your jars carefully and away from your face.

How to make powder

While powder making is extremely simple, there are a few steps you may want to keep in mind during the process.

STEP 1 –
Set up your space

Make sure you have all tools and ingredients nearby, as you will want to work neatly to avoid contaminating your space with fine dust. Wear proper PPE and measure out your ingredients in advance.

STEP 2 –
Grind and sift your powders

Using whatever method you prefer, process your herbs to your desired fineness, and use a sieve/fine-mesh strainer to sift the powders into uniform blends.

STEP 3 –
Add fragrance

If you are adding essential oils, mix these into one or two tablespoons of your powder in a small, separate bowl before stirring into the rest of the mixture. This will help you evenly add the oil to the powder, avoiding clumps and separation.

STEP 4 –
Clean your workstation

Use water to clean your workstation because it's an enemy to powder, turning fine, fluffy preparations into muddy mixes, and clumping your powders into hard stones. However, since powders can be easily inhaled, it's essential to clean up with water after using them. Liquids neutralize the risk of inhalation, trapping powder and making it easy to wipe away. Whether you're cleaning your tools or wiping up chalk sigils from your ritual floor, make sure to use water or cleaning liquid to make this process simple and safe.

As with all botanical preparations, powders are safe to make and to use as long as the practitioner is knowledgeable to take proper precautions. With these tools at hand and notes in mind, powder-making should be one of the simplest magical crafts in this book. Many of the recipes ahead are recreations of historical magical powders, while a few represent my own crafting and experimentation, coming directly from my own grimoires. As you move through this chapter, which employs powders to create magical dusts, powder-potions, and ritual chalks, please keep these notes in mind, and enjoy exploring this historical and oft-overlooked method of magical herbcraft.

SCRYING POWDER

Many witches are familiar with Tarot, pendulums, and runes as forms of divination, but scrying is a method with an even deeper history. While Tarot originates from 15th-century Europe, records of scrying practices are recorded in Ancient Egyptian and Greek religions, and even mentioned within the Bible. This practice involves both sight and discernment, requiring the practitioner to both look for shapes within their selected media, and then discern the meaning of the symbols that appear. While scrying upon oil, smoke, and crystal balls are the most iconic examples, scrying into herbal powders cast upon water has its place within the witch's workshop as well.

We are working with one poisonous plant, the yew tree, so it is best to powder these herbs while wearing a mask. The amount of yew we are using in this recipe is nowhere near enough to cause harm, but taking precautions is always the best practice. You may elect to remove the stems from your yew if they are too woody to process. This recipe can be crafted at any time, but pay close attention to the movements and aspects of the Moon, as she is the ruler of divination and second sight. Crafting on a full moon when she is free from negative astrological aspects, or even on divination holidays like Midsummer and Halloween, would be ideal.

Makes: about 10g/0.25oz powder
Prep time: 20 minutes

FOR THE POWDER
* 1 tablespoon mugwort
* 1 tablespoon yarrow
* 3 small branches of yew, about 8cm/3in each
* 1 tablespoon opopanax resin
* Electric spice grinder
* Sieve/fine-mesh strainer

I Very finely powder your herbs and resin. Because this recipe calls for a fine grind, an electric spice grinder may be the best choice for processing your herbs. Sift these powders through a fine-mesh strainer before combining.

2 Prepare your scrying vessel with clean, fresh water. Any dish capable of holding water will do, no matter how large or small. If you have never scried upon water before, you may want to experiment with light, dark, or clear vessels, to determine which materials give you the best results. For example, I love scrying in light-coloured ceramic dishes, like teacups, as this allows the shadows of the powder and the ripples upon the water to be easily seen.

3 Find a quiet place to meditate and prepare your questions. Speak your question aloud, then take a pinch of the scrying powder and scatter it over the surface of the water. You may choose to stir with the little finger of your left hand or allow the powder to move freely. Pay close attention to any clearly defined shapes that emerge and let the lines and curves of the powder suggest various symbols to you. These images may not be immediately apparent, but like images in clouds, the mind will naturally find a recognizable shape.

4 Record all symbols that you see, regardless of whether they feel important at the time. Unlike Tarot, where cards have clearly defined meanings, scrying is a nonlinear practice, and requires a foundation in both occult symbolism and attention to one's own personal arcana of images. While it is important to study symbolic language so that we can master it, your individual associations and feelings about certain symbols will always be more relevant than definitions found in books. Use these various tools to determine an answer to your question, either at the time of the reading or later, while reviewing your reading notes and researching the images you received.

RITUAL CHALK

Chalk is a staple of many magical workings, particularly within ceremonial magic traditions. These operations often require the magician to work within elaborately drawn matrices of symbols, and using chalk as a writing medium has many benefits here. It is affordable, easy to source, and easy to remove after the ritual is complete. It can write on almost any textured surface, and can be made of 100 per cent natural materials. This recipe adds a few magical ingredients to basic chalk, particularly those that are known for enhancing magical work of all kinds. While spell-specific chalks can certainly be made, this formula is great for making a large batch of all-purpose magician's chalk, enough to last a full year or more.

Makes: about 20 sticks of chalk
Prep time: 30 minutes, plus 3–5 days drying

FOR THE POWDER
* 120ml/4fl oz/½ cup moon water (see below)
* Newspaper/disposable covering
* Face mask and gloves
* 3 hazel leaves
* 1 tablespoon frankincense resin
* 1 tablespoon dried vervain
* Grinding and processing tools (see page 28)
* Mixing bowl
* 225g/about 1 cup plaster of Paris
* 30 drops essential oil fragrance (optional)
* Silicone chalk mould
* Towel

1 Begin by making your moon water if you do not have any on hand. Leave the water under the light of the full moon, with recitations of praise for the moon or her goddesses, then gather the water at dawn the following day. Because water is perishable, this should be used immediately or frozen until ready to use.

2 Prepare your workstation. Cover the surface in newspaper or a disposable covering, and work using a mask and gloves. Care should be taken to work neatly within this area.

3 Finely powder all herbs and resins.

4 In a mixing bowl, stir these powders into your dry plaster of Paris until evenly mixed. Add the moon water slowly, bit by bit, until evenly incorporated, stirring to remove all lumps. If you want to add an essential oil fragrance, do so at this stage, stirring until the oil is absorbed by the wet plaster.

5 Carefully pour this plaster mixture into your mould, tapping the mould upon your surface occasionally to level the plaster. Tidy up all plaster and powder with a wet towel when complete. Allow to stand for 1–2 hours until firm enough to unmold, then dry at room temperature for 3–5 days until fully dehydrated. Store in a dry place, enclosed in a bag or Tupperware to limit damage and dust.

6 Use this chalk for drawing sigils and magic circles on all textured surfaces, such as floors, trees, walls, and doors, and on any surface that works for ordinary chalk.

ATTRACTION BODY POWDER

The use of cosmetics for magical purposes has a very ancient history, beginning with magical perfumes in the ancient world. Cosmetics have, for most of human history, been luxury items reserved for an elite class who can afford them. However, after the Industrial Revolution, mass-market cosmetics and fragrances became accessible to common people, and naturally became subsumed as magical tools within their traditions. In American hoodoo, we see this very clearly with the use of eau du toilette like Florida Water and Hoyt's Cologne, and even magical body powders like this one here. While this recipe does not come from the hoodoo tradition, it is inspired by the subtle glamour of cosmetics magic, and explores a unique way of working attraction magic that is affected through a person's physical presence alone.

It is best to carry out this ritual on a Friday at a Venusian hour, when the moon is waxing. Work in silence, with a drop of honey or pinch of sugar on your tongue, until the powder is completed.

Makes: 60g/2.25oz powder
Prep time: 20 minutes

FOR THE POWDER

* 1 tablespoon cubeb berries
* 1 tablespoon dried rose petals
* 1 tablespoon dried lemon balm
* Grinding and processing tools (see page 28)
* Sieve/fine-mesh strainer
* Mixing bowl
* 20 drops essential oil fragrance (optional)
* 25g/1oz/¼ cup cornflour/cornstarch
* Airtight jar

I   Finely powder all your herbs. As this recipe will be worn upon the body, a finer powder will be more comfortable, so it is best to sift your herbs as well to avoid any larger pieces.

2   Draw a symbol of Venus upon your work surface in lipstick or red ink, like the one pictured here.

3   Place your mixing bowl atop this symbol and combine your ingredients in the bowl.

4   If you are using an essential oil fragrance, place your oils in a small separate bowl, then add cornflour little by little until the oil is absorbed, working out any lumps that form. Stir the cornflour mixture into your powdered herbs and mix evenly to combine.

5   As you stir your ingredients together, you may finally open your mouth to recite orations to Venus, sing songs of love, or read poems of desire and longing. This is both an offering to Venus, the ruler of poetry and song, and also an act of Venusian consecration.

6   When finished, transfer your powder to an airtight jar, and store upon your Venus altar or near the mirror you use to get ready every day.

7   To use, dust your body lightly with the powder using a soft brush. This is best employed before promising dates, job interviews, media appearances, or any occasion where your charisma and magnetism could use a magical boost.

MEDIEVAL DANCING POWDER

The Petit Albert is a fascinating grimoire from medieval France. It is filled with familiar entries from other contemporary works, such as planetary and word squares, as well as a plentitude of folk charms and sympathetic spells. Of its many, many charms for love, *The Petit Albert* contains one most curious rite, employed using powder. Like many other charms from the same time, this spell emphasizes herbs that are gathered on St John's Day, 24 June – a day regarded in the magical calendar for picking and processing especially potent magical herbs. Herbs should be gathered after the sun sets but before the following dawn on the eve before St John's Day. The text specifically says that these herbs should be picked fresh and then "dried in the shade" – meaning they are dried very slowly and without the harmful radiation damage of the summer sun – particularly the wild herbs that are emphasized within the text. The herbs are then powdered and used to encourage partygoers into revelry, specifically to excite young women into voluntarily dancing topless.

This French text certainly begins to sound a bit like Mardi Gras, but the charms employed in this spell are pretty common for the era. What is notable here, however, is that the powder is meant to be employed upon the entire party, blown or scattered into the air such that it could be breathed in by the revellers. While the spell does have a specific target in mind, it is enacted upon not just the people of the party, but the entire space that the party takes up. The text contains other notes about the setting as well, suggesting that the party must be jolly, lively, and lit by lamps burning the fat of a hare and a young goat. Of course, women must also be present to dance! We can think of this spell as creating a sacred space, with the powdered herbs acting upon the entire arena of the party to enhance and draw forth desires and tendencies that are already present. The text suggests that if the mood is right and the party is popping, this spell will be "infallible". Craft this powder for yourself and get a taste of medieval French debauchery.

Makes: 20–25g/0.75–1oz powder
Prep time: 20 minutes

FOR THE POWDER

* 2 tablespoons dried marjoram
* 2 tablespoons dried thyme
* 2 tablespoons dried verbena
* 2 tablespoons dried myrtle leaves
* 3 dried walnut leaves
* 3 small stems of fennel, dried
* Grinding and processing tools (see page 28)
* Sieve/fine-mesh strainer

1 Very finely powder your dried herbs so that they can be employed discreetly and without notice. Pass the powders of each herb through a sieve/fine-mesh strainer before combining.

2 When the moment is right, fling the powder into the air, or sprinkle upon a charcoal brick and burn as incense.

ANOINTING POWDER

This recipe takes its inspiration from the cults of Vesta within Ancient Rome. Within this tradition, a preparation called *mola salsa* (meaning "salted flour") was prepared by the blessed Vestal Virgins, the chaste priestesses of Vesta's temple. Vesta is an interesting figure within Ancient Roman religion, in that she personified both the hearth of the home (the seat of everyday sustenance and survival) and also the national hearth fire of the Roman state, linking together ideas of food, fire, and national identity within one goddess figure. As such, this sanctifying powder was used at important rituals, particularly dusted upon the foreheads of those who were being led to sacrificial death. For some festivals, this mola powder was mixed with water to form unleavened wafers similar in style to the Christian Eucharist.

While grain flour might sound uncommon as a magical ingredient, there is so much precedence for its use in purification and sanctification rituals. Wheat paste and bread doughs have been considered good and pure offerings to spirits since the ancient world, with many traditions even crafting effigies of their gods in bread, as it was likened to living flesh. In Ancient Mesopotamia, magic circles were even drawn on the ritual floor using grain flour, particularly in rituals to invoke personal gods or to perform exorcisms. Even St Hildegard Von Bingen, a medieval abbess and doctor, writes in her medicinal handbook *Physica*[xiii] that there is "nothing lacking" in wheat flour, which she viewed as medicinally and spiritually "full of profit".

While only the holy virgins were allowed to prepare this recipe in Ancient Rome, modern practitioners can take hold of these ancient tools themselves. If you want to be very particular and traditional, perhaps a period of ritual purity (chastity, fasting, and prayer) should be held before the creation of your own *mola salsa*. This recipe should be ground fresh from whole emmer wheat berries, which contain both the bran and the germ of the wheat. Freshly ground flour has a limited shelf life of 6 months and can occasionally draw pests, so it's best to make this recipe in small quantities.

Makes: 80g/2.75oz powder
Prep time: 20 minutes

FOR THE POWDER

* 65g/2.5oz wheat berries
* Grinding and processing tools (see page 28)
* Sieve/fine-mesh strainer
* 1 tablespoon sea salt
* Airtight jar

I Lightly toast the wheat berries in a pan over a medium heat, or in the oven at 180°C/350°F/Gas for 8 minutes. Set aside to cool.

2 When cooled, the grains can be powdered and sifted, along with the salt, which should be ground as fine as possible. Since wheat berries are quite dense, a spice grinder will greatly assist here.

3 Store in an airtight jar/container.

4 To use as an anointing powder, sprinkle your mola upon any items which are being given over or dedicated to the gods and spirits you work with, such as offerings, sacrifices, statuary, and altar spaces. Using small, discreet amounts is perfectly fine, but because this is not a cooking recipe, there is no "correct" amount to use. This work is greatly aided when offerings and chants to Vesta are made as the powder is mixed, as she is the divine progenitor of this recipe, and the Roman guardian of all magic that occurs within the kitchen.

LOVE POTION POWDER

When we think of potions, most of us probably conjure the same mental image: the mysterious vial of liquid, potent and alluring, that can be slipped clandestinely into the drink of our unsuspecting beloved. It's an iconic image, and while many liquid potions did exist in history, the love potion powder was equally ubiquitous, if not more so. These pulverized herbs could be dissolved in food or wine to achieve the same result, and since they do not employ any extractions of plants, the flavour was usually more subtle. While many love potion recipes from history feature animal ingredients and poisons like powdered snake heart and datura flower, this recipe focuses on accessible, safe herbs which are called upon as potent allies in love magic. To craft this powder, begin when the moon is waxing or full, and in a Venus-ruled sign like Libra or Taurus.

Makes: 30g/1oz powder
Prep time: 20 minutes

FOR THE POWDER

* 1 tablespoon dried damiana
* 1 tablespoon ground cardamom
* 1 tablespoon dried jasmine flowers
* 1 tablespoon dried apple blossom
* Grinding and processing tools (see page 28)
* Sieve/fine-mesh strainer
* Mixing bowl
* 3 tablespoons powdered sugar
* Airtight jar

1 Finely powder and sift all of your herbs, working to achieve the finest grind possible. In keeping with traditional examples of love magic, you may wish to add a touch of your personal concerns to this mixture, such as a drop of honey that has been swirled upon the tongue.

2 In a mixing bowl, stir your powdered herbs together with the sugar until evenly blended, working out any lumps.

3 Store this powder in an airtight jar, labelled with a symbol of Venus.

4 To use as a potion, sprinkle a small pinch of powder into the food or drink of the one you desire. To fortify established romances, consider willingly ingesting this potion alongside your beloved. Keep in mind that, unlike a culinary recipe, this powder does not need to be administered in large, palpable quantities. In fact, subtlety is often key in love potions, so small, clandestine pinches will be more than enough.

POWDER OF THE SEVEN FLOWERS

This special recipe comes to us from the Greek Magical Papyri or PGM, a collection of papyrus documents on magic and spellcraft from late antiquity. It features in a few different charms, employed to various ends – it's sometimes used as incense in initiatory rituals, sometimes compounded with resins into a more complex burnable blend, and in one notable case, it's used to make ink which can then be washed away and drunk as a potion, so that the spell can be taken very literally into the body. However, because lily, daffodil, and wallflower are toxic to ingest, this final method is not recommended for modern practice. Nonetheless, this charm is significant because of the number of plants used, which is the same as the number of classical planetary spheres worked within Greek and Roman magic. While celestial associations aren't given for these flowers within the text, they feature alongside a list of seven planetary incenses, leading some to infer a correlation.

To prepare this powder for yourself, begin on or just before the full moon. This is specified within one entry of the PGM concerning the powder of the seven flowers but is not necessarily required. The text also mentions that these herbs should be worked fresh and macerated together before being dried as a paste. This presents challenges for the modern magician, as some of these herbs are seasonal and difficult to acquire all at once. If you'd like to take a traditional approach, you may work these herbs fresh or rehydrate them with a small amount of water before pulverizing. If not, dried herbs work just as well. For the less accessible plants, where they cannot be picked fresh by the magician themselves, they can usually be found in grocery stores, flower shops, and certainly online. There is much about ancient magic that needs to be adjusted for a modern world, and so these small historical inconsistencies must sometimes be forgiven.

Makes: 10g/0.25oz powder
Prep time: 20 minutes

FOR THE POWDER

* 1 teaspoon dried marjoram
* 1 teaspoon dried lily
* 1 teaspoon dried lotus
* 1 teaspoon dried thyme
* 1 teaspoon dried erysmium (wallflower)
* 1 teaspoon dried daffodil
* 1 teaspoon dried rose
* Grinding and processing tools (see page 28)
* Sieve/fine-mesh strainer
* Mixing bowl
* Airtight jar

1 Ensure your flowers are dry before beginning.

2 Finely powder all ingredients, and pass each through a sieve.

3 Once they are properly powdered, combine the ingredients in a mixing bowl, and stir until evenly blended.

4 Gently transfer the powder to an airtight jar. Before sealing, pray over the mouth of the jar. You may choose any prayers you like, but perhaps an invocation of the seven planetary spheres or to Flora, the goddess of flowers, would be appropriate. Seal the jar and store for future use.

5 This powder has many uses in its original context, but typically as an ingredient in larger, more complex workings. This powder can be dusted upon candles, sprinkled on the hands before ritual, or used in consecrating talismans. If you choose to burn this powder as an incense, please do so in a well-ventilated area, as some of the ingredients are mildly toxic. You may choose to employ this blend when performing work which calls upon all of these powerful spheres, such as initiatory rites, consecrations, and powerful sanctifying works of all kinds.

RITUAL CIRCLE POWDER

Ritual circles occur in many traditions throughout human history. They are drawn upon the floor in a variety of media (typically powder-based) as a proper container for the work at hand. As such, no recipe for ritual circle powder can ever truly be all-purpose, as each ritual will require the magician to carefully curate the "arena of reception" for their work, so that spirits, divinations, visions, and blessings can be properly received. However, this recipe compiles a collection of herbs that are associated with increasing both magical potency and the intensity of visions, which can certainly aid most magical operations. Additionally, this recipe involves the addition of a magical ingredient – a sigil, representing the magician's path – which personalizes this charm to the witch who crafts it.

It is best to perform this work under a full moon when the moon is in Gemini or Virgo. These signs are ruled by Mercury, the planet which governs magic and manifestation. For this reason, it is also best to work within a Mercurial hour if possible.

Makes: about 60g/2.25oz powder
Prep time: 20 minutes

FOR THE POWDER
* 30g/1oz sandalwood powder
* 4 tablespoons dried vervain
* 4 tablespoons dried mugwort
* 4 tablespoons dried elderflower
* 2 tablespoons dittany of Crete
* 2 tablespoons dried wormwood
* 2 tablespoons copal or opopanax resin
* Grinding and processing tools (see page 28)
* Face mask
* Mixing bowl
* 1 small square of paper
* Airtight jar

1 Finely powder your herbs and resin. For ritual circle powder, our herbs need not be so fine, so sifting is not necessary here. However, because we are working with powdered woods, it is best to craft this recipe while wearing a protective mask.

2 In a large mixing bowl, stir these powdered herbs together until evenly combined.

3 On a piece of scrap paper, work out a sigil that represents your personal practice. This can be a traditional symbol from your lineage, a personal glyph, or whatever you wish – the point is that the symbol be representative of who you are as a magician. Once the sigil is formed, copy it onto the small square of paper, and hold this over your bowl of powder.

4 Set the paper alight and burn until it is reduced to fine white ash.

5 Stir this ash into the powder until all ingredients are homogenous, then store in an airtight jar near your altar or ritual space.

6 While this recipe was originally intended to be used to draw ritual circles, this is only one application. Use this powder to mark seals and symbols onto your ritual floor, to dust petition papers and magical tools, and in all forms of magic dedicated to work within the Mercurial sphere. Because these ingredients are all natural, this recipe also works for outdoor rituals, and can be used in natural spaces where chalk will not work, such as upon soil or grass.

CLEANSING SALT

Cleansing magic is given over and over again by modern witchcraft traditions as one of the first and most important skills for new witches to develop. This is nothing new; even ancient magical traditions emphasized purity and spiritual cleanliness, and even pre-described particular acts of cleansing to be undertaken before any ritual began. In many of these traditions, salt is used as a cleansing and purifying ingredient par excellence, most likely because of its nature as a natural preservative. Black salt is coloured with another natural detoxifier, charcoal, adding depth to the sympathetic correspondences in this blend. In our recipe, this classical purifier is combined with other powerful cleansing plants, particularly those used in exorcism rites and the cleansing of physical objects and spaces. Cedar, frankincense,

and hyssop trace their origins as cleansing herbs to the Bible, while juniper and St John's wort are used this way in European medieval folk magic. As a combination, this recipe invokes some of the most powerful and well-regarded cleansing herbs in the witch's cannon.

Like all forms of cleansing magic, this recipe is best prepared on the waxing or new moon, when the moon is in Aries or Scorpio. These signs are ruled by Mars, the planet of boundaries and protection, thus making them useful allies for the Moon, who rules purification and the stewardship of innocents. If you cannot source black salt easily for this recipe, sea salt will work just as well, but steer clear of iodized salts and Epsom salts, as they may not be suitable for all applications.

Makes: 580g/1lb 3oz salt blend
Prep time: 20 minutes, plus 1 hour infusing

FOR THE POWDER

* 6g/½ cup lightly packed cedar fronds
* 4 tablespoons dried St John's wort
* 4 tablespoons dried hyssop
* 1 tablespoon frankincense resin
* 4 tablespoons dried juniper berries
* Grinding and processing tools (see page 28)
* Mixing bowl
* 2 tablespoons high-proof grain alcohol
* 550g/2 cups black salt
* 50 drops juniper berry essential oil (optional)
* 50 drops cedar essential oil (optional)

1 Powder your herbs and resin.

2 In a mixing bowl, stir these powders together thoroughly until evenly combined.

3 Stir in the alcohol, then allow the mixture to stand covered for 1 hour. This step liberates the essential oils and fragrances from the plants very effectively, extracting the alchemical "spirit" of the plants into the alcohol.

4 When an hour has passed, stir in your salt and essential oils, if using.

5 Use this salt in cleansing baths, in the purification of ritual tools, in personal cleansing rites, cord-cutting magic, in the breaking of a ritual fast, or strewn upon the floor after rituals are complete. For kitchen witches, this recipe can also serve as a beautiful botanical finishing salt, but be sure to leave out any essential oils if you intend to use it in cooking. This salt adds a touch of herbal flavour, especially when used as part of simple meals, like buttered bread or bone broth.

Further Resources

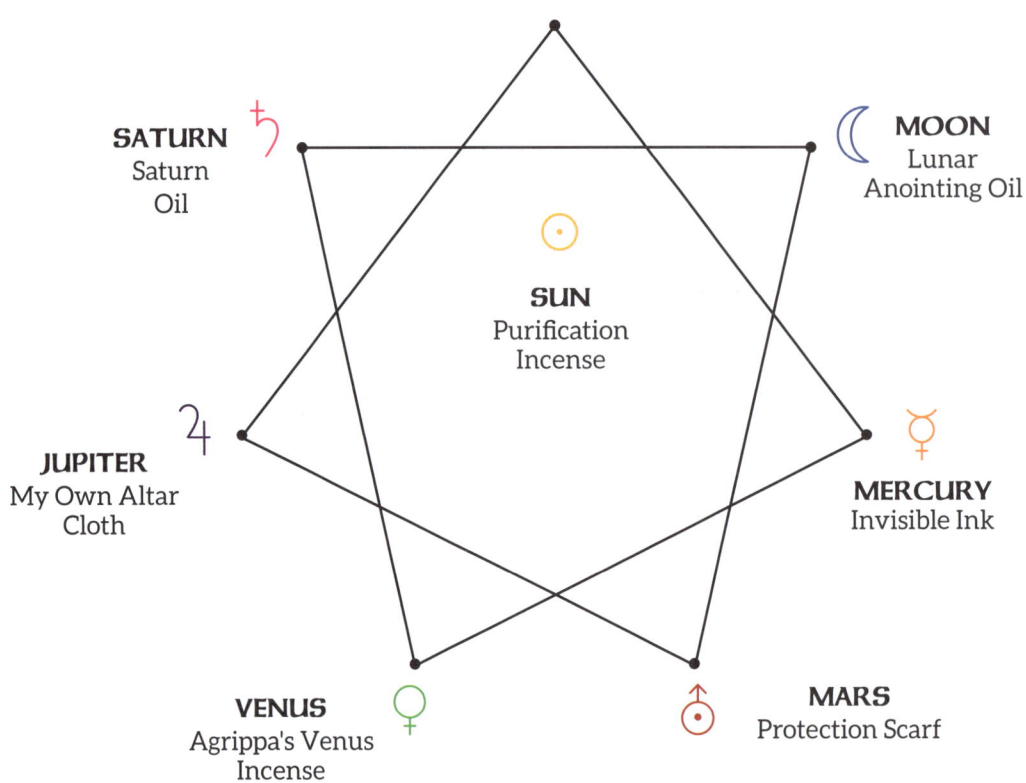

SATURN ♄
Saturn
Oil

MOON ☽
Lunar
Anointing Oil

SUN ☉
Purification
Incense

JUPITER ♃
My Own Altar
Cloth

MERCURY ☿
Invisible Ink

VENUS ♀
Agrippa's Venus
Incense

MARS ♂
Protection Scarf

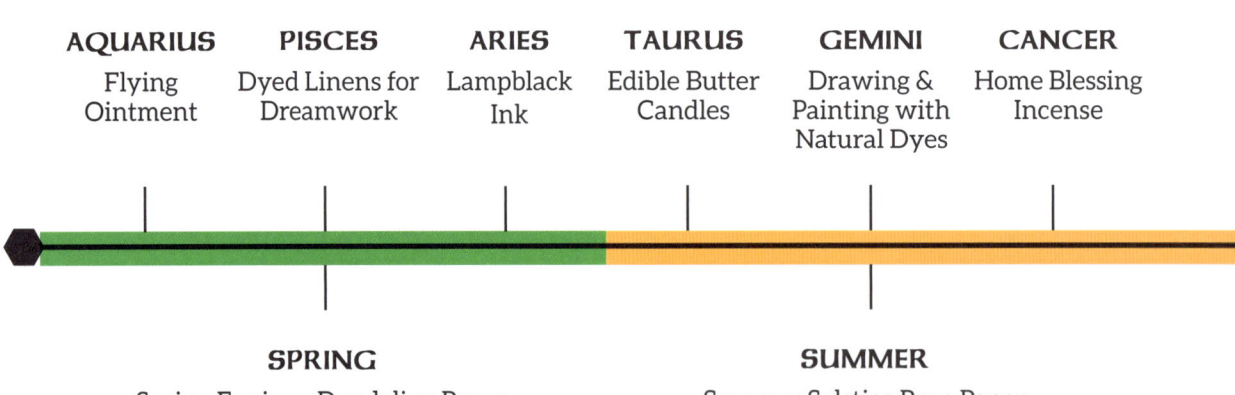

AQUARIUS
Flying
Ointment

PISCES
Dyed Linens for
Dreamwork

ARIES
Lampblack
Ink

TAURUS
Edible Butter
Candles

GEMINI
Drawing &
Painting with
Natural Dyes

CANCER
Home Blessing
Incense

SPRING
Spring Equinox Dandelion Paper
Spring Equinox Ritual Tablecloth
Incense of the Green Spirit

SUMMER
Summer Solstice Rose Paper
Naturally Coloured Candles
Tapputi's Royal Calve

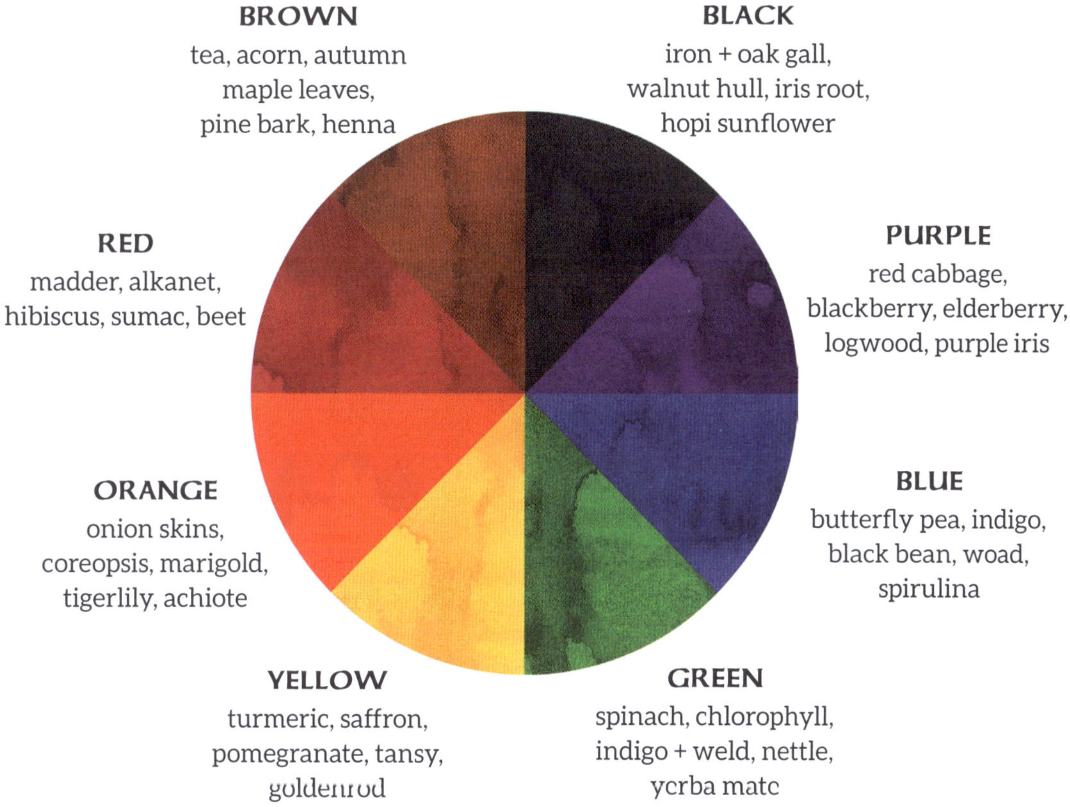

BROWN
tea, acorn, autumn
maple leaves,
pine bark, henna

BLACK
iron + oak gall,
walnut hull, iris root,
hopi sunflower

RED
madder, alkanet,
hibiscus, sumac, beet

PURPLE
red cabbage,
blackberry, elderberry,
logwood, purple iris

ORANGE
onion skins,
coreopsis, marigold,
tigerlily, achiote

BLUE
butterfly pea, indigo,
black bean, woad,
spirulina

YELLOW
turmeric, saffron,
pomegranate, tansy,
goldenrod

GREEN
spinach, chlorophyll,
indigo + weld, nettle,
ycrba matc

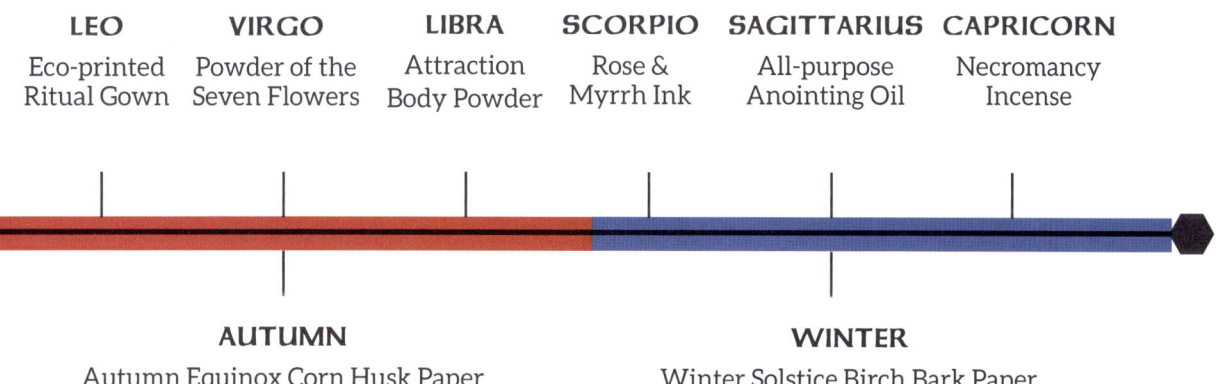

LEO	VIRGO	LIBRA	SCORPIO	SAGITTARIUS	CAPRICORN
Eco-printed Ritual Gown	Powder of the Seven Flowers	Attraction Body Powder	Rose & Myrrh Ink	All-purpose Anointing Oil	Necromancy Incense

AUTUMN
Autumn Equinox Corn Husk Paper
Dipped Candles
Snake Blood Ink

WINTER
Winter Solstice Birch Bark Paper
Mullein Torch Tapers
Ritual Chalk

ABOUT THE AUTHOR

Melissa Madara is a witch, herbalist, educator, and author living in New York City. They are the head of Moon Cult, an online organization dedicated to sharing quality education and resources on witchcraft, occult history and the botanical arts. Melissa's research centers on the folklore and pre-christian religions, with a particular focus on finding historical formularies for food, fragrance, and herbcraft. Find their features in *The New York Times*, *Vogue*, *Vice*, or follow Melissa's published works in *Fiddler's Green*, *Venefica Magazine*, and their debut recipe book, *The Witch's Feast*.

As an occultist, Melissa's practice is largely concerned with the ancient religions of Eastern Europe and the Mediterranean coast, divination, herbal magic, and work with poisonous plants. Their research deals primarily in plant folklore, mythology, and historical formularies, with a particular interest paid to culinary recipes and fragrance. As an herbalist, their work with incense, perfume and tinctures can be found under Melissa's apothecary brand, Moon Cult Herbs.

References and Further Reading

REFERENCES

[i] Hans Dieter Betz, *The Greek Magical Papyri in Translation*, The University of Chicago Press, 1986

[ii] Abraham of Worms, *The Book of Abramelin: Revised and Expanded*, translated by Georg Dehn, Nicolas-Hays, Inc Publishing, 2015

[iii] Aleister Crowley, *The Book of the Law*, Red Wheel Weiser, 2015

[iv] Heinrich Cornelius Agrippa, *Three books of occult philosophy written by Henry Cornelius Agrippa of Nettesheim ... ; translated out of the Latin into the English tongue by John French*, London, printed by R.W. for Gregory Moule, 1651

[v] Aleister Crowley, *777 and Other Qabalistic Writings of Alesiter Crowley*, Red Wheel Weiser, 1986

[vi] Johan George Hohman, edited by Daniel Harms, *The Long-Lost Friend: A 19th Century American Grimoire*, Llewellyn Publishing, 2012

[vii] Edited by Joseph Peterson, *The Sixth and Seventh Books of Moses*, Ibis Press, 2008

[viii] John Michael Greer and Christopher Warnock, *The Picatrix*, Adocentyn Press: 2010

[ix] *The Book of Abramelin*, sacred-texts.com/grim/abr/abr076.htm

[x] Heinrich Kramer and James Sprenger, translated by the Rev. Montague Summers, *The Malleus Maleficarum of Heinrich Kramer and James Sprenger*, Dover, 1971

[xi] Albertus Parvus, translated by Tarl Warwick, *Petit Albert*, Ouroboros Press, 2013

[xi] Michael R Best and Frank H Brightman, *The Book of Secrets of Albertus Magnus: Of the*

[xii] *Virtues of Herbs, Stones, and Certain Beasts, Also a Book of the Marvels of the World*, Red Wheel Weiser, 2000

[xiii] Hildegard Von Bingen, translated by Bruce W. Hozeski, *Hildegard's Healing Plants From Her Medieval Classic Physica*, Beacon Press, 2001

FURTHER READING

Daniel A Schulke, *The Green Mysteries: An Occult Herbarium*, Three Hands Press, 2023

Corinne Boyer, *The Witch's Cabinet: Plant Lore, Sorcery, and Folk Tradition*, Three Hands Press, 2021

Rebecca Beyer, *Wild Witchcraft: Folk Herbalism, Garden Magic, and Foraging for Spells, Rituals, and Remedies*, Simon & Schuster, 2022

Aiden Wachter, *Six Ways: Approaches and Entries for Practical Magic*, Red Temple Press, 2018

Paul Sedir, *Occult Botany: Sédir's Concise Guide to Magical Plants*, Inner Traditions, 2021

Paul Beyerl, *A Compendium of Herbal Magick*, Phoenix Publishing, 1998

Stacey Dugliss Wesselman, *The Home Apothecary: The Cold Spring Apothecary's Cookbook of Hand-Crafted Remedies & Recipes for Hair, Skin, Body and Home*, Quarry Books, 2013

Index

Note: page numbers in bold refer to illustrations.

WATKINS
1893

The story of Watkins began in 1893, when scholar of esotericism John Watkins founded our bookshop, inspired by the lament of his friend and teacher Madame Blavatsky that there was nowhere in London to buy books on mysticism, occultism or metaphysics. That moment marked the birth of Watkins, soon to become the publisher of many of the leading lights of spiritual literature, including Carl Jung, Rudolf Steiner, Alice Bailey and Chögyam Trungpa.

Today, the passion at Watkins Publishing for vigorous questioning is still resolute. Our stimulating and groundbreaking list ranges from ancient traditions and complementary medicine to the latest ideas about personal development, holistic wellbeing and consciousness exploration. We remain at the cutting edge, committed to publishing books that change lives.

DISCOVER MORE AT:
www.watkinspublishing.com

Read our blog

Watch and listen to
our authors in action

Sign up to
our mailing list

We celebrate conscious, passionate, wise and happy living.
Be part of that community by visiting

f /watkinspublishing   X @watkinswisdom
▶ /watkinsbooks   ⬡ @watkinswisdom

Chamomile
Field thyme
Rosehip
Big plantain
Chamomile
Field thyme